Other Hawksmere Reports and Special Briefings published by Thorogood:

Influencing the European Union
Peter Wilding

Managing Corporate Reputation
Simon Scott

Practical Techniques for Effective Lobbying
Charles Miller

Public Affairs Techniques for Business
Peter Wynne-Davies

Techniques for Ensuring PR Coverage in the Regional Media
Mike Imeson

Insights into Understanding the Financial Media – an Insiders View
Simon Scott

Published by Thorogood Limited

12-18 Grosvenor Gardens

London SW1W 0DH.

Thorogood Limited is part of the Hawksmere Group of Companies.

A CIP catalogue record for this Briefing is available from the British Library.

ISBN 1 85418 192 0

Printed in Great Britain by
Print in Black, Midsomer Norton.

A HAWKSMERE SPECIAL BRIEFING

Corporate community investment

How to make your business profitably popular

By Chris Genasi

PUBLISHED BY THOROGOOD LTD

THOROGOOD

THE PUBLISHING
BUSINESS OF THE
HAWKSMERE GROUP

For Grace and Louis

Acknowledgements and thanks

I would like to thank the following for their time, their openness and their advice during the writing of this publication:

- Sara Tye, Head of Press and Public Relations at Yellow Pages

- Charlotte Hines, Senior Research Executive at MORI

- Dian Vandenburg, Marketing Director at Countrywide Porter Novelli

- Susan Wilkinson, Fundraising Director at The National Trust

- Gordon Roddick, Co-Chairman at The Body Shop

- Geoffrey Bush, Director of Corporate Citizenship, Diageo plc

- Mike Love, Vice President Director of Communications at McDonald's Restaurants Ltd

- Jackie Holman, Head of Investor Relations at Railtrack

- Louise White, Director of Public Affairs at Camelot plc

- Michel Ogrizek, Head of Corporate Relations and Bob Harcourt, External Relations Manager at Unilever plc

- Dominic Fry, Group Communications Director, J Sainsbury plc

- Robert Beckett, Development Director at the Institute of Social & Ethical Accountability

- Patrick Chapman, Head of Corporate Partnerships at the World Wildlife Fund

- Colin Byrne, Chief Executive of Shandwick Public Affairs

- Linda Ruggiero, for her help with charts and graphics.

About the author

Chris Genasi has over 13 years experience of public relations. His specialism is the management of corporate reputation and he has advised several leading multi-national companies including Nestlé, Lever Brothers, Toyota Motor Corporation, Castrol, BP, Allied Domecq, Courtaulds Fibres, Rolls-Royce Motor Cars and BT.

He is a Director of Shandwick Welbeck where he is responsible for the company's Corporate Division. Chris has particular expertise in: communications strategy development, internal culture change programmes, issues management, corporate media relations, opinion former communications and corporate citizenship activity.

Chris began his career in market research before moving into PR consultancy and retains a strong interest in the use of research and evaluation in PR. He is a member of the Account Planning Group, the International Association of Business Communicators, The Institute of Social and Ethical Accountability and the Institute of Public Relation's City and Financial Group. He also sits on the Consultancy Management Committee of the Public Relations Consultants Association, as well as the Corporate Responsibility Group and The Council of the Institute of Public Relations.

Contents

The next big thing

The rise of the good corporate Samaritans

Corporate community investment (CCI) – it's a reputation thing

One company's CCI is another's sales promotion

chapter 1

Chapter 1:
The next big thing

The rise of the good corporate Samaritans

Supporting good causes is big business. In 1998, British industry spent an estimated £171 million pounds on helping charitable causes - from providing discrete philanthropic donations to high profile cause related marketing schemes.

There is no doubt that this is an area of growing interest in the business community. It has become a highly fashionable subject in the constant search for competitive differentiation in an increasingly homogenised world, occupied by ever wary, cynical and fickle consumers.

This briefing is a guide for business people who want to get the most out of this area. It is first and foremost designed to be a practical guide for managers who are planning and running campaigns which involve a good cause or which have a community element.

The recommendations are based on:

- In depth discussions with major corporations plus leading charities and advisors in the field

- Quantitative research - specially conducted for this briefing - with over 40 companies into practices and attitudes.

- Many discussions with leading figures from this sector and over 12 years of personal experience of consultancy work for companies such as Allied Domecq, Toyota Motor Corporation, Lever Brothers and Nestlé

Corporate community investment (CCI) – it's a reputation thing

The observations made in this briefing, start from the basis that a company's involvement with good causes is essentially a reputation-driven issue. It is true that many philanthropic donations are made by companies, Foundations and Trusts, where no recognition is sought. However, this form of donation is not what is covered in this briefing.

Instead we are looking at what is typically called corporate community investment (CCI), which is most frequently carried out to meet specific business goals and to reflect the doner company's values and beliefs.

Expressing these values through CCI is always linked to a company's reputation, in the sense that if the CCI is successful, then the company will be well thought of and if the company is well thought of, its business goals will be easier to achieve.

One company's CCI is another's sales promotion

Companies that are successful in their CCI, add dramatically to their competitive edge. To give two of the most well known examples: The Body Shop's global business was built largely on its support of causes; Tesco's Computers for Schools campaign builds loyalty in one of the most competitive sectors of British industry,.

But these two companies approach the issue of CCI very differently. The Body Shop's values are what drives its CCI. It is a CCI led business to a great extent. As Co-Chairman, Gordon Roddick says, 'supporting causes and issues is part of our corporate DNA'.

Tesco's Computers for Schools, on the other hand, is a sales promotion. The fact that it is linked to a popular (with consumers and the government) cause, reflects well on Tesco; but it does not – in the same way as with The Body Shop – say anything fundamental about Tesco as a corporate citizen.

Both these examples are similar in that they are both very successful and popular with consumers and hence help to make those companies more successful and profitable.

But follow very different routes to arrive at the same destination. This emphasises the difficulty of knowing what is the most effective route for companies to pursue in gaining maximum value in this field.

This briefing aims to provide some guidance and looks at how companies can lift their CCI activity from being a grafted-on, minority interest to something that delivers a whole range of business benefits, by making CCI part of the culture and spirit of the company and its brands.

What is CCI?

chapter 2

Chapter 2:
What is CCI?

One of the difficulties of discussing this area is that the phrases used mean different things to different people.

Corporate community investment – or 'corporate community involvement' as it is sometimes called – covers the support of good causes by a company, or by a brand.

However, this interpretation is open to a very broad range of meanings. Talk to a chief executive of a major company or a corporate affairs director and you may well find the conversation covering the areas of corporate ethics, environmental responsibility, fair trade, employee relations, consumer affairs and fairness at work.

Talk to a marketing director and you are more likely to cover building brand loyalty, cause related marketing, or developing brand equity and affection among consumers.

The human resources director will think of internal communications and staff motivation; and the local factory or store manager will start talking about local schools, councils and government officials.

A fund manager or analyst will probably equate CCI with ethical investment.

The fact is that CCI applies to all these audiences. And it is not just about supporting charities or good causes. When used to its fullest potential, it can define a company's personality, build employee loyalty and help create a forcefield of goodwill that will cushion a company in times of crisis and threat.

CCI is more than just 'impact on society'

CCI is just one of the elements of corporate citizenship. Good corporate citizenship is all about how well a company behaves and conducts itself in society. This incorporates all aspects of a company's financial, physical, social and environmental impact.

A good corporate citizen should aim therefore to:

Produce the maximum profit possible, by offering the best possible goods and services at the lowest possible price, using the least amount of resources in a sustainable way and providing safe and pleasant working conditions in an environment which respects and develops individuals, while providing them with a fair financial reward.

By fulfilling these attributes any company would be making its maximum contribution to local and national communities, directly through wealth creation, employment, and the provision of goods and services which improve the quality of life. By simply being a good company, any business will make a significant contribution to society.

Importance of CCI and Corporate Citizenship

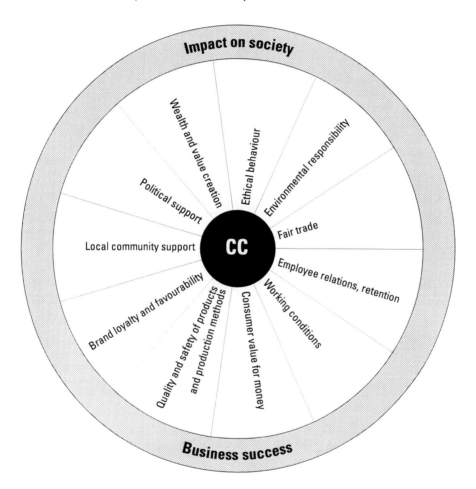

Isn't that enough?

A company that is achieving this level of business conduct would indeed be a paragon, but for many forward thinking companies, being a good business in traditional terms, is no longer enough.

Increasingly companies are thinking more laterally about their role in society and how they can work within the communities in which they trade in order to improve those communities and derive benefits for themselves in the process.

This is where modern corporate community involvement comes into play. CCI is therefore a tactic to be used as part of a corporate citizenship strategy. It can be used as a way of enhancing and promoting a company's success – for example in the area of environmental protection. Alternatively it can be used to create a more fulfilling environment for employees or to create brand differentiation.

However, whatever aspect of CCI is used, it is typically designed to enhance the overall corporate citizenship of a business, which is in effect enhancing its overall performance financially and in every other regard.

Many businesses will be familiar with the European Foundation for Quality's Business Excellence model. Most companies tend to see CCI as only contributing towards the 'impact on society' set of scoring. However, forward thinking companies are recognising that in fact corporate citizenship affects and informs all parts of the Business Excellence Model. If good corporate citizenship equates to being a good business, then corporate citizenship will drive such other areas of the Business Excellence Model as 'leadership', 'people satisfaction', 'customer satisfaction' and so on.

Companies that recognise that being a good corporate citizen means being a good company, will have begun to have changed how they look at the world. By changing their view of what they need to do to survive, such companies become what I describe as 'inside out companies'

Inside out companies

Not every company recognises that good corporate citizenship equates to good business practice and excellent financial performance. Most managers still see making maximum profit at the opposite end of the scale from good corporate citizenship.

A cartoon in the FT famously lampooned this view, with a meeting of company executives and one of them saying: 'The balance sheet shows that doing good adds to the bottom line, but not as much as doing bad'.

'Good guys come last' is still the prevailing business culture and generally managers believe that improved performance in the area of corporate citizenship will lead to either direct or indirect costs.

However, the evidence is overwhelmingly against this view. Almost without exception, the world's greatest and most enduring corporations are those that realise that by being a good corporate citizen – along the very broad lines described above and including such fundamentals as quality products at competitive prices – you delight every stakeholder (internal and external). And when every stakeholder's needs are met, the profits start to flow.

Evidence to support this view is considerable. I am grateful to the Future Foundation for highlighting the following:

- A 20 year study by Kotter and Heskett of 200 companies showed a clear correlation between long term profitability and corporate cultures that express the company's purposes in terms of all stakeholder relationships

- The famous briefing *Built to Last* by James Collins and Jerry Porras found that clear values and an inclusive approach were characteristic of long lasting and successful US corporations

- Ethical trust funds have grown and are seen to be outperforming the market in many cases. Also Kleinwort Benson was recently reported as having set up an inclusive company fund, reflecting the above average performance of such companies.

What is being highlighted above is the success of companies that put stakeholders at the centre of their business. In other words, groups that are seen as outside the company are put at the centre. It is this revolutionary approach which typifies the inside out company.

All too often managers feel the need to run the business in a way that sees all audiences other than shareholders as 'outsiders' all looking to take profit and dividend away.

Forward thinking companies recognise that they need to put the consumer at the centre of their business, so they begin to run their businesses inside out, by which I mean they see every stakeholder as being able to add value to the business as long as they are included in the dialogue upon which business decisions are made.

Inside out companies are transparent in their dealings and stated aims – they take their internal conversations and communicate them externally. In effect such companies say the same things internally as they do externally and as a result there is no 'deception' of the consumer and the company can legitimately position itself as being on the side of the consumer.

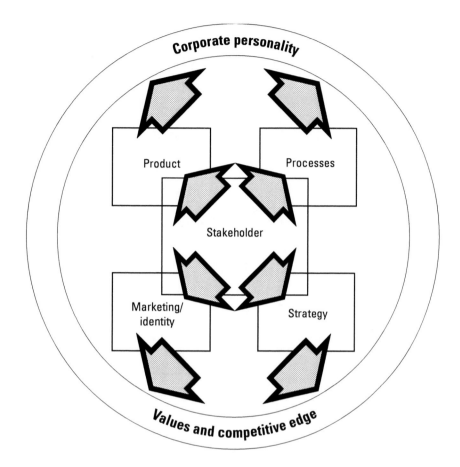

Companies such as Dyson Appliances, ASDA, Virgin and The Co-op are all typical inside out companies and have achieved competitive edge and favourable reputations by convincing the public and the media that they are consumer championing organisations. And in a world where most companies are seen as faceless monoliths, such a 'human' positioning is immensely powerful.

Inside out companies turn all their thoughts about company structure around, placing stake-holders in the centre.

Inside out companies realise that they have no right to exist and that they will only be able to continue trading and attracting employees and capital, if they listen to their stakeholders and give them want they want and what they value.

Types of CCI

There is a very wide range of ways that companies can get involved in CCI. Many companies will use several techniques to meet different needs. In this section, I have listed some of the most commonly used tactics and tools and given an indication of their merits and when they might be most appropriate.

Later in the briefing I will explore the other factors that a company should take into account when looking at which of these tools would be most helpful. This will include which sector a company operates in, the target audiences involved, the competitive environment, business needs and available resources.

Philanthropy

This is where a company will provide a simple cash donation to a good cause. The decision to make the donation will normally be made by a committee of individuals who will look at the cause and make the award if it feels the cause is deserving. The committee members will typically include non-company representatives and often the donation is made via a foundation or a trust fund.

Most foundations or funds will give money to support specific themes – e.g. the family, environment, young people etc. In addition to an appeal having the correct theme, Foundations may also have other well-defined criteria – for example, the good cause may have to raise matched funds, or need to be self funding after a period of time.

Characteristic of most donations of this kind, is that they are not directly or overtly linked to the company behind the donation. The donation is made because the good cause is seen as worthy of support. It is not a donation made as part of furthering the business goals or values of the donor company.

Normally the donor seeks no public recognition or publicity benefit from the donation, although there is normally rigorous demands made of the good causes to justify that the donation is well utilised.

In many cases donations are made by trusts or foundations established by wealthy individuals or by individuals within a company. The Sainsbury Foundation is a good example of a philanthropic body which has no connection with J Sainsbury the company, although it clearly shares the name. However, a number of the Sainsbury Foundations have made the step of 'Debranding' themselves and removing the Sainsbury name from their official title.

When might a company consider philanthropy?

Corporate philanthropy in its purest sense is, by all accounts, a declining form of corporate giving. In today's business world where everything must be justified, measured and be seen to be adding to the bottom line, virtually anonymous donations that are not tied to business goals and which are not designed to raise the profile and reputation of the business, are seen as an inappropriate way of spending shareholders' money. This is the reason why many philanthropic donations are made by wealthy individuals, who only have to answer to their own personal desires to make a contribution in ways that suit them.

However, there are occasions when a company might think about philanthropy as an appropriate route forward. Probably the most high profile example is Camelot's decision to establish The Camelot Foundation. The lottery operator, hit by adverse media coverage of its profits and senior salaries, felt the need to be seen to be conducting its CCI to the highest standards of integrity.

The company therefore elected to create a separate entity – the Camelot Foundation – to allocate and administer its corporate donations. Clearly the company looks to derive reputational benefits from the Foundation, and does inevitably influence its behaviour to some extent (the Camelot Chief Executive sits on the Foundation Board for example). However, the Camelot Foundation does provide a distance between the company and its donor arm, which brings a rigour and sense of propriety, which is essential for a business such as Camelot which has been subject to media and governmental criticism.

If Camelot had run its own CCI scheme, there could have been a media backlash. The Foundation gives a greater sense of independence and detachment, making such attacks harder to sustain.

Other companies that may benefit from a foundation or trust style of philanthropic giving, could be those companies in controversial markets – tobacco, nuclear fuel, or genetically modified crops for example – where the company may want to establish some distance between its public brand and its philanthropic activity.

Cause related marketing (CRM)

Cause related marketing is a relatively new phenomenon in the UK. Although it has been used since the early sixties, it is only in the last 5 years or so that it has really burgeoned, thanks largely to the efforts of Business in the Community, which has been promoting CRM very actively and seeking to establish good practice guidelines for companies and charities operating in this area.

Essentially, CRM is a sales promotion device, whereby a company will agree to give a donation to a good cause, if a consumer buys their product or service. Tesco's Computers for Schools campaign works in this way: consumers spending over a certain amount will receive a voucher which can be collected by schools and exchanged for computer equipment.

CRM can be broader than providing simply a set amount or percentage of a sale price as a donation. Some companies develop special products which trigger donations to good causes if selected by the consumer. One of the most notable examples is Pizza Express's Venice Pizza, where a donation is made to the fund set up to save Venice every time this particular pizza is sold.

Many companies develop special Red Nose versions of their products for the bi-annual Comic Relief appeal, again with all or part of the sale revue being given to the cause.

Other initiatives exist whereby space on a product's packaging or delivery vehicles might be donated to a good cause. Examples include the New Covent Garden Soup's on-pack promotion of the issue of homelessness, or The Body Shop's use of their vehicles to publicise missing persons details.

While these variations exist, most CRM is about linking company donations to sales.

When might a company consider CRM?

CRM is undoubtedly a useful tool to be used to increase sales and improve reputation. However, it must be used with great care. Business in the Community publishes detailed guidelines, but the key points for successful CRM relationships are as follows:

- Select a cause that is relevant to your brand/company values and attributes. There needs to be a fit between the cause and your business, otherwise the consumer becomes confused and suspicious. Inappropriate marriages between companies and causes at best lead to the supporting company being relegated to corporate wallpaper – a faceless sponsor that nobody can remember. However, at worst, inappropriate partnerships will arouse suspicion and risk a backlash, with consumers and the media viewing the company's involvement as entirely cynical and manipulative of the good cause.

- Recognise that a partnership between a company and a charity will require openness, honesty and a considerable investment in time to ensure that it is a true partnership and that the full benefit is felt.

- Put on your blackest hat and look for possible risks and issues that the most aggressive investigative journalist would seize upon – for example, if you are supporting disability issues, what is your company's own policy like on providing employment for disabled people.

- Be sensitive in your communications – no body is expecting you to support the good cause for the sake of it, but there must be a judgement based on 'good taste' as to the extent and style to which a CRM initiative is promoted. One of the most high profile examples of a CRM initiative which was considered in poor taste was Flora's support of the Diana Memorial Fund, through its donations based on purchases of packs of Flora – in especially redesigned packaging to highlight this link.

- In itself, the CRM campaign for Flora was a good idea, raising large sums of money for this good cause. However, it was judged to be in poor taste to use Diana's signature on the pack and more generally, to link margarine sales to this whole area, was seen as over commercialisation and not relevant to the brand.

- Ensure that the money being raised will be used for a specific need and will not disappear into a black hole. Understand what difference the money will make as it may well be essential to justify your spend to the media at some stage.

CRM is potentially the most sensitive area of CCI as it typically operates with a very high profile, involving a large numbers of people. It brings the world of good causes and commerce together in a very overt way. Anything that is high profile brings risks, so thorough crisis planning and risk assessment is essential.

However, high profile activities can also bring major benefits for those companies willing to conduct CRM campaigns. Typically companies will guarantee a donation to the good cause regardless of sales of the product. Companies should bear in mind, that the cost will be at a certain minimum level, regardless of sales. Secondly, companies must understand that CRM is still ultimately a donation – companies cannot simply increase the price of a product to cover the cost of the CRM. CRM offers the consumer a discount, which is passed on to the good cause. The expense of this discount will be a cost for the company. Naturally the aim is that the increase in sales will exceed the amount of the donation required, both in terms of increased profits and in terms of product trail.

CRM is clearly well suited to fmcg brand marketeers, looking to build a warm personality around a brand which extends beyond its existing attributes. CRM is typically supported by marketing departments and will usually be implemented by a sales promotion company and overseen and promoted by a PR consultancy, who are vital to help foresee and prepare for issues, as well as promoting the scheme in a positive way to consumers.

Employee volunteering

Encouraging employees to volunteer to help charitable initiatives or good causes, is an increasingly popular route for CCI. Typically employees would be encouraged to spend time working with good causes, either of their own choice, or suggested by the company.

This type of activity needs to be developed closely with the human resources department of any organisation, as it will impact on available time at work and could be linked to the human relations strategy. For example, involvement in good causes could be used to support a strategy to foster a stronger sense of unity between employees across a large company or group of companies.

In such a case, employees from different parts of the organisation could be organised to work together at a local charity or at a local school, for example. Similarly, departmental teams could be organised to work together in this way.

The benefit of bringing employees together in this way is that it can build team spirit and morale. Similarly for individual employees, company assisted volunteering can be a way for employees to enhance their job satisfaction. For example, a manager may find it highly rewarding to pass on his or her managerial and business skills to a local community project looking to raise funding.

The local charity may not have the expertise or resources and will benefit greatly from the employee's expertise. For many employees, their time as a volunteer proves very rewarding and can enhance their loyalty towards their employer, who is seen as the benevolent provider of this opportunity to make a difference.

Some companies provide very clear guidelines as to which good causes should be supported and arrange volunteering options in conjunction with a charitable partner – eg The Prince's Trust, who can arrange for volunteering schemes to be organised across the UK.

Other companies will ask employees to nominate local charities that they wish to support. Railtrack, for example, offers a combination of the two. The company has preferred causes and charities for local support, but there is also a separate fund to provide matched funding to charitable causes suggested by employees.

It is also increasingly common for companies to offer incentives in this area. Typically these take the form of:

- A set number of paid days off per year for employee volunteering
- Including volunteering in personal appraisals, with employees being rewarded in career terms for their involvement in local communities.

Three to five days off per year appears to be the most common allowance in large corporations. Increasingly lean workforces, however, puts considerable pressure on employees' ability and willingness to commit additional time to work-led volunteering. Similarly, staff that work on shifts may find it practically difficult to get involved in the community during normal working hours.

Nonetheless, a significant percentage of people will probably already be doing some voluntary work. Many will be helping out with school fundraising, local hospices, and other local charities. Also the experience of many companies is that today's busy life and work styles, actually may lead to more people wishing to volunteer to help good causes, as a contrast to the relentless drive for commercial goals. For many, it makes a refreshing contrast to do something for people who may be from a very different background and set of circumstances than an employee might normally encounter.

When might a company consider employee volunteering?

Employee volunteering can be very effective if a workforce has a strong affinity to the location where they work. If the workforce commutes long distances, then there is often less community spirit than say a factory that draws its workforce from a smaller, more local geographic area.

Employee volunteering should be offered as one of the options available that a company will support rather than the only CCI option. Essentially this is something that will suit some employees but not all. Rather a company should put out clear messages that it supports this activity and that it can help anyone looking to get involved. It should be encouraged but not made to feel mandatory.

Employee mentoring

Employee mentoring is a type of volunteering, but one which operates at a more personal level. What normally happens is that an employee or group of employees, will be matched with a specific good cause, and will be asked to work closely with that cause and to share knowledge, experience and provide encouragement and support.

This can range from listening to a schoolchild read once a week, working with a family that has a disabled child to provide help around the home, or spending time with an unemployed young person, helping them to prepare their CV and job interview skills. Another example, might be for a group of managers to work with a local school, or community group on developing a business plan to attract more funding.

There are many examples of mentoring taking place and this is another growth area for CCI. The benefits are that it allows employees to become committed to good causes for a sustained period of time. Also the intimate nature of mentoring means that there is often a clearer link between the help provided by the employee and the results gained by the recipient – essentially it is easier to see how that employee has made a difference.

When might a company consider mentoring?

Mentoring is especially appropriate when the workforce is relatively small and would benefit form a strong focus being developed on their behalf. The tailor made nature of mentoring means that employees can build schedules to suit their timetables, whereas 'straight' volunteering may be less flexible in this regard.

Like volunteering, mentoring can be highly rewarding for the individual and allows a company to direct its employee involvement with greater clarity than a mass volunteering scheme might allow.

However, also like volunteering, companies should not rely solely on mentoring. Instead it should be encouraged and made accessible and easy for people to get involved.

Mass employee involvement

Both mentoring and volunteering are fairly sophisticated methods and they may not be appropriate for all circumstances. Companies should also look at easier and simpler ways to involve employees.

Probably the simplest is to establish a Give As You Earn scheme. This is the most painless way for employees to donate through their employer. Regular feedback on the causes supported by GAYE and the amounts raised will help to encourage this form of CCI.

Other forms of employee involvement include one off events. The most obvious occasions when employees might be organised to support good causes would be for Children In Need, the BBC's annual appeal and for Red Nose Day, organised every two year's by Comic Relief.

However, companies could consider organising their own parallel versions of events which unite people in support of good causes. McDonalds and Allied Domecq are just two corporations that hold company wide days or weeks when all employees are encouraged to raise money for good causes. Head office can provide local ambassadors for such events with fund raising ideas and merchandise such as posters, balloons, T shirts, standard press material etc, in order to help local companies or branches to organise their own event. In such cases it is important to provide adequate methods for activities to be well recorded – eg the amounts raised, people involved, charities supported etc.

It can be very helpful for such days or weeks to be themed to support a common cause – eg homelessness, local healthcare, health and fitness. The broader the theme, the more likely that local operations will be able to tailor their preferred local causes. A national charity partner can be established, but experience shows that local branches or operating companies are more likely to respond if they can choose local charities or causes to support, under the central umbrella theme.

Many companies opt for a combined approach – offering the national charity as one to support unless a suitable local cause is preferred.

Mass employee involvement is most likely to succeed if it takes place over a concentrated period of time – a week is normally better than a single day. This allows for employees to plan around existing time commitments.

When might a company consider mass employee involvement?

This is especially useful when there is the desire to create a strong sense of unity amongst employees. A high profile, focused week of activity is also very useful to attract support from local media and local politicians, who can be involved in events and photocalls.

Companies might also consider mass employee involvement if the business is widely dispersed around the UK – a large multiple retailer, for example. However, large scale employee events are suitable for single site and smaller companies too. They remain popular tools for employee involvement in CCI, and should typically be offered as a high profile element within a mix of employee involvement options, including individual volunteering and mentoring schemes.

Grant distribution

The awarding of grants for good causes can be a highly effect way for companies to make CCI contributions. Many companies offer grants – ranging from a few hundred pounds to several thousand – to organisations such as schools, local charities, community groups or individual/teams in sport, the arts or areas such as personal development or regeneration.

The best of these schemes, will award grants against clearly defined criteria and in support of specific themes. Typically these themes will reflect a key attribute of the company. For example, Toyota was traditionally a major supporter of science and engineering in the UK, reflecting the core competencies of Toyota itself.

It is vital to have a clear set of criteria to judge applications for grants. This helps to deter non-relevant applicants, and ensures the selection process is efficient and fair.

Many schemes look for recipients to raise funds equivalent to the grant award, as part of the qualifications for the grant – known as 'match funding'. Other schemes insist in partnership between the recipient and other related bodies. For example a school will receive a grant if it links up with a local enterprise.

Many grant award schemes are run by a charitable body on behalf of a company to assess initial applications for suitability to receive support. Other companies might use a charitable body not only to judge the applications, but then to administer the grant and provide monitoring and evaluation of the funded initiative against agreed criteria. Companies must be willing to fund an intermediate charity for this service with both cash and resource to assist the charity.

However, this is usually a very modest cost – perhaps 10 per cent of the total grants awarded and provides an essential service, which the company would do well to contract out to experts in this field.

When might a company consider grant giving?

Awarding grants for specific good causes is especially appropriate when a company is seeking to support an area that reflects its commercial interests or core values. Once set up, grant award schemes are one of the simplest forms of CCI, yet they can also be highly effective.

Therefore, grant award schemes might be appropriate where a company has limited in-house resources to manage CCI – for example where there is no dedicated Community Relations Manager.

The potential disadvantage is the lack of hands on involvement by the company and hence the potentially reduced chance for employee involvement or for more in depth PR benefits. However, well thought through grant giving schemes will look for ways that the donor company can be integrated in the process – eg by involving managers in grant award ceremonies, or inviting selected grant winners to corporate events, or ensuring adequate branding at grant receiving locations.

In summary, grant awards are most akin to the traditional styles of corporate philanthropy, when a cheque is simply written by a company to help a good cause. However, forward thinking companies will make this approach work harder for them, by ensuring:

- High profile relevance of the grant to their business or brand values and key messages

- Active integration of the company in the selection of grant winners and in the communication of the grant programme

- Smart companies will also look to support themes and causes that are newsworthy and popular with their target audience, whether that be customers, employees or political figures.

Donations of equipment

Companies should consider donating equipment which may no longer be of commercial value to the company but which is still perfectly usable for an organisation such as a school, or a local community group. Outdated computer equipment is probably the most frequently donated item – assisted by the endless stream of new computer developments, which render machines obsolete within months of purchase.

However, other items could be donated – old databases or directories of industry figures for example. Outdated (slightly) data on markets and trends could be very valuable for a voluntary group looking to raise funds.

Paper that has only been used on one side, office furniture, out of specification products, seconds, excess stock, space on delivery vehicles – all can be usefully donated by companies.

There are three key points to bear in mind when a company donates equipment or materials:

- Ensure the equipment or product is safe for use or consumption

- Provide adequate training or instruction for the use of the donation

- Keep an accurate record of the items donated. This will help when the total CCI value is calculated. As well as recording the number of items donated, it is useful to record a cash equivalent value. An estimation should be made as to the value of the donated items if they were purchased by the good cause on the open market. Do not forget to include the value of delivery and of training to use the product if relevant.

Donations of pro bono work

Donation of employee time is largely covered under the sections on volunteering and mentoring. However, some companies –particularly professional services firms such as PR agencies, advertising agencies, management consultancies and law firms – may also donate their professional services without charge. This is known as pro bono work.

However, it may not be only professional services firms that offer pro bono work. Builders have been reported offering their services for free to help construct houses in the developing world, doctors will perform medical tasks free of charge in poorer countries.

As with donating equipment, it is critical that the pro bono services provided are delivered to the highest standard to avoid charges of exploitation and to ensure that the good causes receive the best possible support.

Companies looking to provide pro bono services therefore need to agree strict parameters for what will be provided. Companies should deliver what they have promised to their normal high standards, but not set unrealistic goals or offer vague levels of support.

When might a company consider pro bono work

Pro bono activity can benefit a company by adding to its credentials and providing stimulating career opportunities for employees. Some advertising agencies do their best work for charities – often for no fee. Similarly PR companies will help good causes to promote their campaigns. This form of activity can help put the providing company on the map, especially if the cause is high profile. The resultant case study can then be used to attract other clients.

Companies may wish to consider pro bono work, therefore, where the workforce is highly unlikely to involve itself in a volunteering or fundraising activity and is most likely to respond to the idea of using everyday work skills to help worthwhile causes.

Like other employee schemes, some consultation with staff about what scheme to support is advisable, but this should also be balanced by direction on suitable themes from the company itself.

Seedcorn funding

Similar to straight grant giving, seedcorn funding from companies to good causes differs in that seedcorn funding implies considerably more work from the recipient in preparing the application for funding than might be the case for a one off grant.

With seedcorn funding, the company is acting more like a venture capitalist or business angel, and providing an amount of funding for a good commercial or community idea. The seedcorn funding could be very large and would typically be dependent on a detailed business plan showing why the funding should be awarded and then what the long term plan is for the good cause to maximise the funding – ideally as a basis to become self funding.

Effective schemes in this area will be long term partnerships, where the company will often retain an interest in the funded venture for some time

When might a company consider seedcorn funding?

The company may have a particular desire to encourage enterprise among good causes or with disadvantaged or excluded groups and individuals. In which case, seedcorn funding would meet the dual goals of CCI and fostering enterprise.

A smart use of seedcorn funding would be to combine it with employee mentoring. For example, experienced managers could work with community groups, charities schools, local artists, sports people etc to help them develop viable business plans. These would be used to apply for the seedcorn funding, plus money from other sources. Company employees could then continue working with those good causes helping them to grow the seedcorn funding, and develop their enterprise into the future.

Employment opportunities

This refers not to opportunities for existing employees, but rather to ways in which a company can extend employment opportunities to disabled or in some way disadvantaged people.

For example, disabled people could be provided with support and facilities to gain valuable work experience in a company. Similarly, the long term unemployed could be given career experience (New Deal is the most well know example of this approach).

Not only does this activity provide welcome employment and social activity for the employees, but existing staff typically derive great satisfaction and learning from working alongside a more diverse range of people than would otherwise be the case.

Companies can also use this approach to encourage a more inclusive employment culture – for example to establish representative numbers of ethnic or other groups from society.

Clearly such initiatives need to be carried out in conjunction with relevant charity support groups, to ensure the employees are properly catered for in terms of special equipment and personal support. Other areas to consider are transport to and from work, and the accessibility of the work place – stairs, lifts, toilets, eating areas etc. It is also critical to brief the work force fully of these initiatives so that a supportive environment is created.

Fair trade

Fair trade is a major and complex subject, which essentially concerns payment of a fair price and provision of decent working conditions for suppliers and staff of major companies.

Typically it concerns goods manufactured or cultivated in the developing world for sale in the developed markets. However, it can extend to working conditions of suppliers in the domestic market – for example homeworkers, low paid 'sweatshop' employees or agricultural workers in the UK.

Clearly any company needs to consider its policies in this area in terms of how it does business. However, in addition to these, companies may choose to adopt this theme as a CCI focus.

For example, a company may choose to always stock fair trade products or use fair trade products in its staff restaurants. It may also use its public outlets to promote the cause of fair trade. The Body Shop and Oxfam shops are probably the best known organisations to use their premises to convey a campaigning message.

Bridging gaps between the voluntary sector and donors

Companies should also consider a role as a catalyst for supporting good causes rather than simply providing donations in cash or kind. Companies can use their contacts and expertise to help good causes achieve their objectives, whether that be fund raising or raising awareness.

When might a company consider acting as a bridge?

If a company has limited ability to assist directly, or represents a collective of companies or interests, then the bridging route could be very effective.

For example, a trade association representing many companies, or a shopping centre that is seeking to promote several retail names, could use its position to develop introductions between good causes and its constituent member companies.

Such an approach is not dissimilar to the way groups such as The Rotary Club or The Lions operate in that they represent collectives of companies and individuals, who will assist good causes in a variety of ways, that might not always be in the form of direct donations.

The other occasion when bridge building could be appropriate is when it reflects the nature of a business. Yellow Pages provides a clear fit, but other possible industries that offer bridges between people and organisations would include travel companies, transport firms, or regional development agencies.

Media partnerships

Any CCI will benefit from widespread communication, both to encourage support and to promote a company's involvement in order to enhance corporate reputation.

Unfortunately, as will be covered in chapter six, obtaining media coverage of corporate support of good causes is easier said than done. All too often, the media is only willing to report bad news about business, rather than the details of the positive contribution industry makes both directly through everyday wealth creation and more deeply through the millions donated to communities and good causes all over the world.

As a result of this reluctance on the part of the national media, it is advisable to consider a media partner for any high profile CCI activity.

Remember that any TV, radio or print media operator is primarily interested in attracting bigger audiences. By linking with a good cause, media sales or audience figures may go up, but only if the good cause is popular with the audience and offers an easy way for people to get involved.

A typical example might be a joint promotion with a national newspaper between a branded company and a charitable cause – eg a CRM scheme such as a donation being made if the newspaper and a branded product is bought at the same time, for example.

Alternatively, an appeal might be promoted on television and viewers can call in with donations, which are then matched by the supporting company. Or the media could highlight an issue

and then the supporting company could provide a pack of advice and help on how viewers can support this cause.

As with all commercial or CRM based schemes, high profile media partnerships can bring major benefits in terms of publicity and awareness. However professional legal and marketing expertise must be involved to ensure the scheme is well planned and implemented.

Providing a platform for an issue

Companies can also consider adopting a popular – or even an unpopular – cause or issue and then giving that issue a platform in order to raise awareness, encourage funding or to influence behaviour and attitudes.

The Body Shop used its stores to campaign on Nigerian civil rights issues, Nivea has provided financial support for the issue of breast cancer to be publicised, and Benetton uses its brand to campaign on a whole range of issues centred largely around the need for tolerance and greater understanding of differences in societies.

Clearly this route most suits companies that are highly issues led and associate themselves with agit-prop style campaigns. However, mainstream companies can also benefit from this type of CCI. The main pitfall is that the issue becomes bigger than the supporting company and any corporate benefit or recognition is lost. The other key risk is that the supporting company somehow becomes associated with the issue in a negative – rather than positive – way due to media misrepresentation or consumer confusion.

For example, Unilever's commendable involvement in setting up the Marine Stewardship Council to help protect fish stocks for the future, carried with it the risk that Unilever could have been cited as the cause of overfishing, given its major fish based brands. In fact it is unscrupulous fishing practices that lead to unsustainable fisheries and this was sufficiently well communicated for Unilever to be seen as part of the solution.

However, this remains a powerful route for CCI. If well promoted and clear, it offers companies a single issue to support, which can bring strong benefits for external and internal communications.

Which CCI is which?

Type of CCI	Target audience reached	When useful	Comments
Philanthropy	Good causes	Mainly for individuals, or when distance is beneficial between donor and good cause	Low profile activity – declining appeal for companies
Cause related marketing	Consumer	To boost sales for short periods – most effective when linked to high profile causes	Can provide short term sales lift. Needs caution to avoid consumer/ media backlash and donor fatigue
Employee volunteering/mentoring	Employees, local communities	To provide employee motivation and build loyalty	Requires time intensive involvement – a serious commitment, but very rewarding
Mass employee involvement	Employees, local communities	For one-off, occasional use to unite staff and build morale and loyalty	Needs military style organisation plus resources to match – simplicity and flexibility are essential
Grant distribution	Good causes, consumers, local opinion formers	For companies with limited in-house resources	Charity partner essential. Good planning when establishing a scheme can lead to maximum results, for minimal involvement, although adequate funding will be needed to run the grant giving machine
Donation of equipment	Local community causes	For companies with limited in-house resources	Can involve significant administrative support. Aim to work with charitable partner for ease and effectiveness of distribution
Donation of pro bono work	Good causes and employees	For companies with limited in-house resources	Can be motivational for employees and enhances company credentials. Relatively easy to implement, but can be costly in terms of time and opportunity cost
Seedcorn funding	Good causes, employees, opinion formers	When company values reflect a need to foster enterprise	Works best when combined with employee volunteering. Delivers many excellent news stories and can be highly effective
Employment creation	Disadvantaged/disabled people, existing employees	For companies wishing to build loyalty and morale within the workforce	Simple, effective and valuable for all concerned. Care and resource needs to be allocated to ensure facilities and backup are adequate – explore all costs fully before beginning
Fair trade	Consumers, employees	For companies with relevant values or a target consumer that will be motivated by these issues	Can be a complex issue to support and live up to. May be irrelevant for many consumer groups
Bridging	Consumers, employees	For companies in relevant markets or where funding is limited or not available.	Especially suitable for organisations representing many companies or partners. Can be cost effective way of making a difference without directly funding activities
Media partnership	Consumers, employees	If mass audience reach is required	Will lead to awareness, but will add to cost. Media partner will seek influence and control, which needs management
Platform for issues	Consumers, employees	When a company sees a strategic fit with its business interests	Right for some companies. Cautious approach needed to avoid media and consumer backlash – eg accusations of jumping on bandwagons

What is driving the growth in CCI ?

chapter 3

Chapter 3:
What is driving the growth in CCI?

Don't miss out

Firstly, if you can accept the need to run your company inside out – ie putting the consumers in the driving seat and working to meet their needs – then your business will soon grasp the fact that being a good corporate citizen means being a successful company.

Once a company reaches this point, the value of implementing a CCI programme as one manifestation of good corporate citizenship, becomes irresistible.

Essentially there are two main benefits to implementing a CCI programme:

1. Consumers expect and value it

2. Society increasingly expects it as part of a licence to operate

Changing views of business leaders

It is not just external forces acting on businesses that have led to a growth in CCI. Ever since the publication of the RSA's *Tomorrow's Company* report, business people have been increasingly recognising the need to expand their role beyond the provision of goods, services and wealth.

The rise of organisations such as Business in the Community, the growth in CCI, increased interest in Triple Bottom Line accounting, sustainability and the clear signals from new left leaning, but pro business, governments across Europe and in the US, have all contributed to a shift in thinking within leading corporations.

In a specially commissioned survey for this briefing, corporate affairs directors of over 100 major corporations were asked to answer the question: 'What, in your view, is the role of a company in society today?'

Answers were strikingly consistent. Profits or wealth for shareholders, was rarely given as the sole *raison d'être* for a company. Instead, most felt that a company should combine its role as provider of goods and services and wealth, with a broader contribution to the societies and communities in which it operates.

Two comments which were typical:

'A company should be prepared to support the society from which it makes its profits.'

'We cannot be a truly great company without helping to develop great communities'

However, most remain pragmatic in their view that a company's first responsibility is to provide quality products that people value:

'There is a need to get the basic goods and services right first – that is still what consumers care about most, quite rightly.'

'Community involvement will not cover for poor service.'

From workers' villages to a management discipline

The importance of supporting CCI by business leaders is now part of mainstream thinking. It is not a new phenomenon. Corporate philanthropy dates back beyond the Victorian era.

What is different today is that it has been recognised not just as an altruistic option, but as a useful business tool. CCI is seen as a way to increase sales, build loyalty of employees, win favour with politicians and regulators, and enhance competitive edge through reputational advantage.

Companies are doing what they do best, which is listening to the prevailing mood of stakeholders and responding. CCI is a 'buy stock' and the best companies are making sure they are part of this new opportunity for commercial advantage.

Companies benefit and society gains as millions of pounds are directed to good causes and local communities. Governments benefit as businesses take on a small element of the State's burden – reducing taxes or the need to raise them at least. Employees benefit as companies create opportunities for them to get involved in worthwhile and rewarding activities in their local communities. And the consumer benefits as companies vie to appeal more and more to consumer led agendas.

CCI in its fullest sense, leads to better corporate citizens, which produces more sustainable corporate behaviour, which is good for the planet, for the consumers and for the business itself.

The friendly and healthy levels of suspicion and differing cultural stances of all the partners involved in CCI ventures – such as the media, government, charities and businesses – should act as counter balancing weights, to help ensure that the integrity of CCI remains intact.

As long as CCI is seen as a win-win situation for all partners, then increasing commercial support for CCI will be a beneficial force in society. Charities, NGOs, the media and the public should therefore welcome and encourage corporate participation in helping to tackle societal issues.

So far, companies have acted, in the main, with good taste and integrity, bringing considerable benefit to many communities. The attitudes of business people as revealed in research for this briefing indicate that support for good causes is likely to continue.

Public pressure for 'do right companies'

The media, pressure groups and high profile corporate issues (such as Shell's disposal of Brent Spar and its involvement in Nigeria, pensions mis-selling, the shipwrecking of the Exxon Valdez, and Gerald Ratner's comments which offended consumers) have all led to a consensus among company leaders that corporate reputation matters because:

- The public is interested in the behaviour of companies behind famous brand names

- The media and pressure groups are constantly trying to trip companies up and expose what they see as corporate ills

- The media and pressure groups operate on a global basis, with information being distributed around the world within a very short period of time

- Damage to a company's reputation can cost it millions of pounds in lost sales and make it harder to recruit top talent. A poor reputation can damage or hamper relations with legislators, and will require major investment and resource to rebuild trust in the company and its products

With the exception of some of the financial community this view of reputation and its importance is now well accepted by companies and is no longer seen as a peripheral area of concern.

MORI has carried out the most authoritative research into consumer demands and expectations of companies in this area. The evidence is that the British public remains convinced that companies should do more to help tackle issues, but that their awareness of what companies already do, remains consistently low – albeit with some small levels of growth.

The public call for action

MORI's findings show that two thirds of the British public feel that industry and commerce do not pay enough attention to their social responsibilities. This level of feeling is even more pronounced among the sub-section of the British public that are socio-political activists as defined by MORI (9-11% of the British population).

At the same time there is increasing cynicism and lack of belief among the public that companies' actions are likely to benefit society in themselves.

MORI research shows that over twenty years ago over half of the British public/population do not agree that company success and profits would automatically benefit society as a whole and therefore, expectations for additional evidence of 'socially responsible' behaviour is needed. However, today the situation is reversed, with over 50 per cent of the UK population not agreeing with the view that company success will benefit society as a whole.

This gap between the public's desire for companies to be seen to be doing more in society and the perceived level of actual activity, needs to be filled by higher profiling of CCI activity by companies.

One reason why companies are often loathed to promote their CCI activity more widely, apart from cost, is a concern about a consumer backlash ie, criticism that the company is exploiting its support of good causes for commercial gain.

However, these sensitivities may be exaggerated in the minds of company directors. According to MORI's research of consumers, corporations need not be so reticent in highlighting their support for good causes.

In fact consumers are keen to hear about do right companies, who take their social responsibilities seriously and who are contributing towards the support of local or national issues.

28 per cent of consumers say it is very important to them in their purchasing decisions if they know about a company's activities in society and the community, according to MORI. Furthermore, 28 per cent claim to have – at least once in the last 12 months – boycotted a product on ethical grounds or actively selected a company's products or services because of its good track record in societal or ethical issues.

Perhaps most strikingly, this statistic has increased by 4 per cent of the public between 1997 and 1998 (the most recently available data).

Also, those saying they have purchased a product as a result of its charitable connection – eg via a CRM scheme – has also increased by 2% since 1997.

These are small increases perhaps, but in many sectors, a 2 or 3 % change in purchasing can represent millions of pounds in sales and share gain.

The public's concern with these issues, continues however to be very generalist in nature. Despite claims that this is an area of interest for many, there is virtually no awareness of specific corporate involvement in supporting good causes. With the exception of Tesco's computers for schools, hardly any CCI schemes are spontaneously named in the MORI research.

Ways in which this communications gap can be filled are explored later in this report.

Another disconnect between companies and public perception is in the areas that consumers feel companies should be supporting and those area where they perceive company support to be taking place.

MORI's consumer research shows that companies are often not supporting the causes that matter most to the public. Like the current Government learned, success needs to be based on a thorough understanding of the issues that matter to the people who are your customers.

Aligning a company's support of good causes that are popular not only makes good business sense in terms of reputation gain, but it is more likely to reflect the genuine needs in society, as opposed to a company view of what the issues are.

However, there is also the view that CCI schemes which are entirely consumer and research driven, simply tend to support popular, high profile causes. Virtually every consumer survey will register children, cancer, education, health and jobs as the top priorities. Consumer research led CCI may well contribute to the marginalisation of less high profile or mainstream issues and causes.

Gay related issues, mental illness, concern for the elderly, and ethnic issues are just some of the more complex and less populist causes that will be rarely mentioned in consumer groups.

For a company to solely base its CCI activity on a consumer led agenda is not acceptable if a company wishes to be a truly good corporate citizen. Instead a company should base its activities on a composite agenda, based on consultation with all stakeholders – consumers, employees and also those informed experts in the world of social needs and concerns, who can provide dispassionate advice on where the greatest needs lie.

Only by taking this inclusive approach to CCI will a company really be a do right company. Basing everything on consumer focus groups alone is neither cutting edge nor is it truly the behaviour of a do right company. It is more indicative or a cynical do-what-people-tell-us-will-make-us-look-right company. Not a bad place to start, but certainly not best practice.

Diana, the millennium and the third way

Post Thatcher, post the death of Diana, Princess of Wales, post the election of New Labour and as we move into a new millennium, there is undoubtedly a change in public mood.

Fin de siecle angst, a desire for greater balance between home and work, a move towards a more natural lifestyle that is in balance with nature, a focus on spiritual and personal health

as well as physical and material wellbeing – all these moods and interests make up the cultural, social and political zeitgeist of the late 90's.

Companies who fail to tune in to this new wave of thought risk alienating consumers, employees and failing to attract younger generations – both physically younger and the increasing numbers who are younger in their outlook, values and attitudes.

However, this is not a return of the hippie values of the 1960s. Today's consumer is far more pragmatic and willing to embrace modern commercialism, while striving for a simpler, more fulfilling, natural and healthy lifestyle, within a high tech, corporate society.

Modern consumers accept that companies have their own interests and will tolerate their prosperity only if the deal cuts both ways. For example, consumers will turn a blind eye to high salaries for company directors, will accept premium pricing, will tolerate all manner of things if they feel the company concerned is a do right company.

Anatomy of the do right company

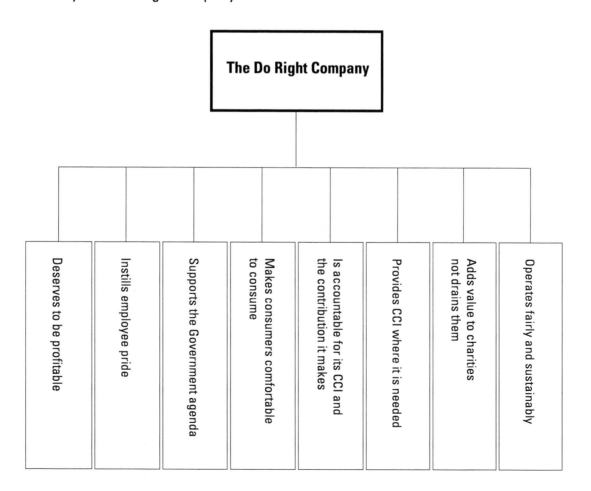

If the business in question is meeting both the material needs of consumers in terms of product quality and value, while also meeting their emotional needs - for example by caring about the well being of the broader society in which the company operates and the wellbeing of people who work for it, buy from it, live near it and make things for it - then today's consumer will endure - even embrace - that corporation.

The days of students wanting to stamp out multi national corporations are long gone. Today we want multi nationals to be here, but only if they put us first - ie run themselves as inside out companies. We want them to produce good products at low prices, and behave themselves in a socially acceptable way.

In many ways, society abrogates its responsibilities to what it determines to be the establishment. In the past it was governments, now it is also corporations that we feel should be guardians of society and the environment.

Of course this is correct, but what is often overlooked is that we are all citizens as well as consumers. We want to be served, but often forget that we too are responsible for our actions.

Whatever the motives, consumers are very understanding of the fact that companies also seek to gain benefit from good deeds. MORI's poll shows that over 60 per cent of the public think that it is acceptable for companies to derive benefit from social and community contributions.

Indeed the research indicates that many are suspicious if companies do not tell people about what they are doing in this area. There is a thirst for knowledge about company support within communities, but the amount of communications activity to serve this need appears to be highly inadequate.

Political encouragement

In addition to public support for companies to be involved in society and community related issues, there is also a very clear lead being given from the Government about what they expect from companies today.

The Labour Government expects companies to make a contribution to the communities from which they derive their profits, customers and staff. Labour is clearly pro business, but they are also expecting business to make contributions to the welfare need.

Who would have anticipated that the UK's first privatised school would be introduced under a Labour administration. The Government, unlike Mrs Thatcher, does believe there is such a thing as society, it is just that they do not believe they are solely responsible for it.

This government sees increasing welfare costs and has been asking companies to consider ways in which they might take on some of these costs.

From selling stakeholder pensions to providing computers and books for state schools, today's government is not too proud to take what the corporate sector can offer. As Tesco puts it: 'every little helps' to reduce the call on public funds.

So far the government is being scrupulous about corporate donations separate from policy making debate.

For example, utilities are active supporters of community schemes, yet this did not stop them being hit by a windfall tax on profits. Camelot is one of the UK's biggest investors in good causes, but when it comes to rebidding for the National Lottery licence, it will stand or fall on its commercial merit alone.

The major supermarkets are still being subjected to an enquiry by the Office of Fair Trading despite their high profile support of charitable causes and contributions to initiatives such as the Millennium Dome.

In the same way that government will not be politically compromised by corporate donations to society, business leaders also have their limits in the extent to which they are willing to be a surrogate to the Treasury in terms of funding essential services.

Currently, a consensus between the state and business seems to have been reached as to the scope and level of investment that is desirable in society.

However, as with the public, many politicians feel that companies are falling short in this area. MORI again offers the most comprehensive research in this area. In their survey among MPs/the House, 83 per cent of Labour MPs felt that industry was not paying enough attention to its social responsibilities. Figures for Conservative MPs stood at 27 per cent who felt not enough was being done by companies.

So not only is Government making it clear they would like business to do more, they are very clear about what areas they would like to see supported.

Many of these are near to home in terms of a company's social responsibility. For example, how a company treats its employees is very important for many MPs. MPs would also like to see companies supporting those areas which are political priorities – education, health, crime prevention, and employment.

Companies which are seen to be supportive of the Government agenda, will not only derive their favour and support in terms of publicity endorsements and assistance in planning, but they will also be directing their CCI to tackle areas of greatest need.

Companies should conduct research with their political stakeholders to identify the priority areas needing support. This could vary if the emphasis is to be local community support as opposed to national.

Once a broad area has been identified – eg education – companies should seek to have meetings with relevant civil servants and charitable bodies in that field to identify in more detail where the needs lie.

For example, if the theme chosen was education, further meetings and discussion might reveal that a key area of need was, say, science education at A level. Further research might reveal that behind this issue lay a poor perception around science as a career. This might lead to a CCI scheme which worked to raise awareness at GCSE level of the benefits of a career in science.

It is this drilling down process in consultation with government officials that often leads to the most effective CCI schemes. Most effective in terms of targeted aid, but also most effective in terms of engaging political support.

This assistance can range from matched funding – for example the Department of Health offers matched funding for health related education schemes sponsored by companies – through to the willingness of Ministers to attend photocalls, event launches and to offer messages of support for CCI initiatives. Other benefits in kind could be envisaged in return for the right CCI package – for example the PR support of the COI, plus mentions in despatches when good practice is discussed.

In this context, it is worth noting another striking figure from MORI's survey of MPs, when asked to state what attributes influence their view of a company as favourable or not.

The ranking of issues of most interest is shown below:

Criteria for judging companies – 1997

Q: What are the most important things to know about a company in order to judge its reputation? (Spontaneous)

	MPs Lab %	Con %	MEPs %
Treatment of staff	67	30	30
Quality of products/services	24	26	34
Financial performance	18	31	26
Quality of management	15	15	12
Customer service	32	32	15
Environmental responsibility	40	23	37
Social responsibility	34	12	34

Source: MORI

There are business people in the cabinet of the current administration and only do right companies are invited to this political party. The door policy is clear. It is populist, ethical and welcoming. For do right companies, there has never been a better time for business to integrate itself in the political and social fabric of this country in a way that is truly of commercial benefit.

Employee needs and pressures

Employees are seen to be one of the most responsive audiences to CCI. Why is this? Of course employees are a captive and obligated audience. They must read company announcements and participate in company schemes if they are to be seen as fully functioning members of the work force. But research carried out for this report, does not indicate that employees are unwilling contributors to CCI schemes.

Most companies report strong levels of interest from their staff to get involved and to make a difference.

Research shows that employees equate a company that is active in CCI terms as probably a better place to work overall. Employees also like to see their companies working to improve

things in society – righting wrongs, making donations to those who are less fortunate and providing support for employees and communities in times of need.

Company research of employees typically shows strong employee admiration for companies that provide organised assistance through schemes such as matched funding, time off for voluntary work and so on.

Employees are citizens too, and nobody wants to feel embarrassed about where they work or the activities of their employer if they are considered unfavourable.

CCI can help address this. In my research, many companies told of how they use CCI to rebuild employee confidence in the company that they work for, following attacks from the media, for example.

Railtrack and Camelot, for example, find that CCI activity involving employees restores pride in the company after a bruising from often unwarranted press criticism.

A company's CCI track record is also useful rebuttal material for employees when grilled by friends and family in the pub, at home, or in other social environments. Professionally too, CCI activity provides ammunition for company representatives to defend the record of their business.

Of course, involvement in CCI activity is often very rewarding in itself for employees. In the same way that consumers are looking for greater balance between the material and the spiritual – between work and the rest of their life – so too are your employees.

By providing them with the opportunity to get involved in this type of activity in a way that is not detrimental to their career or wealth, the employer is seen in a favourable light. All of which builds respect for the company, pride and a sense of loyalty.

This in turn will help with career development, retention rates and in attracting the best people. The direct and indirect costs of a high staff turnover affect virtually every business and virtually all companies are looking to reduce this churn.

Again like consumers, employees are first and foremost looking for stimulating careers, good pay and conditions. However, when these aspects loose their appeal or when there is little to choose between companies as places of work, a well thought through CCI policy can help win over hearts and minds. And when you are in a sector, such as IT or healthcare, where demand for quality staff outstrips supply, then CCI can make a considerable contribution to your competitive edge, by attracting and retaining the best people.

Charities in the boardroom

Another driver for greater CCI is the growing commercialism and willingness of the charitable sector to work with business.

Countrywide Porter Novelli, the PR company, was one of the first to become involved in corporate citizenship related issues and in helping companies to realise the potential of this area of business. Their research into the attitudes of charities toward CRM, reveals the openness and recognition by charities of the need to embrace corporations.

The research shows that cultural differences are being reconciled and that charities are taking full advantage of the rise in interest in CCI. Charities all saw CRM as becoming more important in the future. They also showed an astute awareness of the value of the charity brand. The research demonstrated that charities take a very proactive approach towards evolving partnerships with business. Twice as many charities make the first move towards business than the other way round, and for the majority of charities, the corporate sector has become the largest proportion of their income. No doubt this has been exacerbated by the diversion of public donations to the lottery and to the effect of one off events such as Children In Need.

However there has also been a rise in corporate activity in response to the awakening of interest in CCI stimulated by societal, political and commercial changes.

Research with charities confirms that they see companies as valuable sources of other benefits beyond cash. Helping to raise awareness, attracting volunteers and assistance with one off special appeals are also cited in the Countrywide Porter Novelli research as major drivers for charities in working with the corporate sector.

My interviews with charities for this report have indicated that the honeymoon period may be waning for some partnerships. Typically there is some disappointment at levels of income derived for corporate involvement. However, this seems more a result of hyped levels of expectation around 'new' initiatives such as CRM, which have not turned out to be the big money spinners for charities as many seemed to have believed they would.

If anything, relationships between companies and charities now seem to have moved into a more mature and balanced phase. Expectations on both sides are now more measured. There is recognition that well thought through schemes for joint activity, which are imaginative, innovative and executed with integrity, can derive sustained benefits for both sides.

Ensuring an integrated fit between good cause and company still remains at the heart of a successful partnership – apart from the basics of good communications and written agreements.

A company that is seen to be tagged on to a good cause, enjoys minimal impact in terms of reputation or sales. This is where creativity is so vital. Rather than ram a square plug into a

round hole, PR, sales promotion and advertising creative teams need to work with charity and company to develop memorable campaigns that benefit the cause and the company.

The creative challenge is to make the company and the charity appear to be on the same side of the campaigning fence. To achieve this position of integrity, there needs to be a credible articulation of the company's credentials to support this cause. Otherwise the company is seen as a passive sponsor of the interesting subject being promoted – which is solely associated with the charity and not the company partner.

However, today's charities will understand the commercial need to avoid this occurring and will be very supportive in helping companies feel they obtain maximum benefit, by offering PR support, celebrity assistance and by always including references to company supporters.

Companies should ensure that such support is a negotiated part of any partnership with a charity. The other factor to remember is that forging and maintaining partnerships of this nature takes resource and time. This is often overlooked when CCI plans are made.

Like Government, charities will not compromise their own integrity and brand values to secure funding. But companies will find that the charitable community, like New Labour, is very pro business and they will make it their business to ensure your business obtains value for money from your CCI activity.

The pressure for more sophisticated CCI

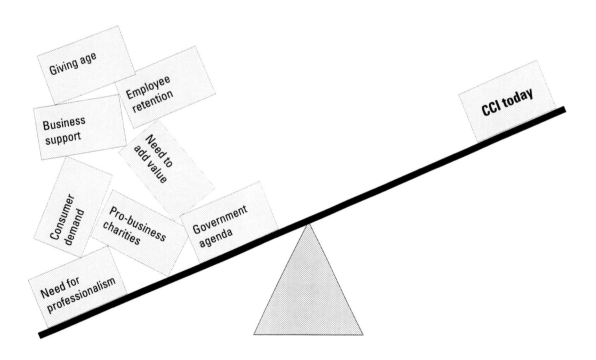

Pressure from the money men

The final area for greater and ever more professional support of CCI comes from what at first seems to be an unusual source. With ever more competitive pressures as a result of globalisation and other factors, businesses are intensely cost conscious and every item of expenditure is closely monitored and rigorously assessed to determine how it adds to the bottom line.

Every area of marketing is scrutinised for return on investment and CCI has also finally come to take its turn under the financial microscope, quite rightly.

The debate continues about if and how CCI contributes to the bottom line in terms of sales and reputation. Ways of measuring its effectiveness are well developed and can be sourced from organisations such as The London Benchmarking Group, the European Foundation For Quality Management, the Institute of Social and Ethical Accountability and Business in the Community. All these organisations can offer expert advice on formal measurement and evaluation systems.

However, the key point here is not about how CCI is evaluated, but the fact that there is so much demand for it to be measured and evaluated, we have seen more and more CCI schemes being developed that add commercial value, whether that be through added sales, improved reputation reinforcement of company values, employee retention or political support.

It has led to the replacement of semi-anonymous philanthropic giving with business led, professional, high profile schemes.

The need to 'professionalise' CCI in order to make it more accountable and acceptable in business terms has led to greater spend in this area (coupled with the effect of the other drivers already mentioned).

Today we typically see 5 per cent of a CCI budget spent on promotion, and another 5 to 10 per cent spent on evaluation. Schemes get bigger and bigger, charity appeals grow larger and larger, causes are never ending, the Millennium acts as a further spur. CCI has entered the realms of other business disciplines. Companies are appointing dedicated staff to run this function and once the process begins, it is apparent that the CCI budget needs to be run effectively, this takes resource, more needs to be done to justify the resource and so on.

Commercial pressure to demonstrate value, will cost money in itself and as CCI becomes ever more sophisticated and is taken more seriously, the scale of the sector has grown accordingly.

CCI – how far can it take you?

Is being a good corporate citizen going to make everything better?

What can CCI do?

How much risk can you stand?

What your marketing style says about you

chapter 4

Chapter 4:
CCI – how far can it take you?

Is being a good corporate citizen going to make everything better?

Being a do right company will improve your reputation, but there is a lot more to being a do right company than simply being active in supporting CCI. Ultimately, doing the right thing may mean getting out of your core business.

For example, it is hard to see how a tobacco company can have a long term future, even though it can have an admirable record as a supporter of CCI and be a good company in operational terms. Ultimately, the impact of its products on the health services and individuals of countries around the world cause more harm than can ever be made up by even the most excellent CCI.

We have seen BP declare its repositioning as an energy company and begin to explore more sustainable sources of power other than oil. BP recognises that long term sustainability means the flexibility to change and adapt to environmental and public pressures in order to maintain commercial viability.

These root and branch approaches are everything to do with corporate citizenship and being a do right company. However CCI alone will not tackle the big issues faced by every company.

So the first point to make is that CCI is useful, but it has its limits. This seems obvious enough, but many companies still see CCI as a substitute for real change. As a way of keeping the barbarians from the gate, by throwing them some sweetened distractions to mask the smell of the real malaise.

This use of CCI as a mask, is typical behaviour from companies that do not embrace the consumer into the heart of the business. The messages going to the outside world are very different to the reality and discussion internally.

Of course, this position is not sustainable for any period of time. Sooner or later, the whistle will be blown by a disgruntled employee or the truth will be unearthed by the media and the game will be up.

The problem is that this type of company is not operating inside out and therefore there is deceit between message and reality. Soon the cracks will start to appear.

CCI cannot rescue a company from a bad situation. The message is simple – get your house in order before starting to take the moral high ground in support of good causes.

What can CCI do?

Having fired a warning shot about the limitations of CCI, let us now look at how it can be effective.

The first thing to consider is how much CCI you need. This depends greatly on a variety of factors: your objectives, size of audience, the number of employees, geographic spread of your organisation, available budget and so on.

Chapter five shows a model to help companies determine the level and scope of CCI needed. This is based on research conducted for this report, which shows that the most popular audience for CCI is employees and that the majority of activity is targeted within local communities.

Companies surveyed reported the following targeting of CCI activity:

The City	2 per cent
Politicians	12 per cent
Opinion formers	12 per cent
Trade customers	2 per cent
The media	12 per cent
Consumers	10 per cent
General public	10 per cent
Employees	24 per cent
Local community	16 per cent

Clearly CCI is proving more effective at reaching some audiences than others. Why is this?

Research shows that great cynicism remains among the media in particular, but also with the general public and City analysts as to the value and worth of CCI.

Typically the media is inclined to report business in an overwhelmingly negative manner. At best the media tends to portray business in a one dimensional way, as solely interested in profits, being something rather detached from every day life and generally existing to make money for its owners.

The stories about business contribution to communities are only really reported in either the regional media – which is generally supportive of the businesses in their communities – and by serious, specialist business publications such as *The Financial Times*, *Management Today* and *CBI News* for example.

MORI and other research among consumers shows that this absence of mainstream positive reporting about business and its support of CCI, has impacted on the public's view of business, which is generally unfavourable, being shaped primarily by business failures or rare, but high profile, cases of bad corporate behaviour.

Consumer affairs programmes like BBC's Watchdog, continue to fuel the public's beliefs that business is out to rip them off. Sensationalist journalism fans the flames of mistrust and does little to empower consumers by making their voice heard in a constructive way that might lead to genuine improvements in consumer service.

Instead companies retreat, having seen that the penalty for trying to discuss issues in the media is public ridicule and media reporting which seeks to drive home an agenda that is wholly anti-business.

Given the media-led distrust of business, it is hardly surprising then that CCI is largely unnoticed, or dismissed as companies trying to buy their way into people's hearts.

All of this means that companies are focusing their efforts more and more on the audiences that are most responsive – employees and local communities, including local political figures and the regional media.

Companies naturally hanker for the perfect CCI initiative: one that appeals to employees, local communities and opinion formers, but which also wins national media support and – most importantly – consumer appeal, leading to more sales and greater brand loyalty.

Tesco's Computers for Schools, is the ideal role model for most corporations. The scheme appeals on every level: to Government because it attacks a real need in society and because education is a top political priority, to local communities because it delivers benefits locally, to consumers as it is easy to support and easy to understand in terms of what it is achieving, it is good for the brand as it supports families – the core target group for Tesco, and it is good for PR as it provides endless regional media opportunities that can involve local politicians, stores and children.

And at the end of the day, Tesco will be able to put a single figure on the CCI contribution – ie x number of computers paid for by y number of vouchers, equating to z amount of groceries bought.

While Tesco's scheme is perfect in every regard, and while many companies would aspire towards such a scheme, it is generally regarded, in the research for this publication, as the exception in the field of CCI. Most businesses do not hope to replicate the breadth of appeal that the Tesco scheme achieves. Instead the prevailing trend is to develop a number of discrete projects that appeal to individual target audiences.

This recognises the very different needs and areas of interest between target groups and the difficulty of creating a 'one size fits all', single CCI concept.

How much risk can you stand?

Another influence in deciding what will be the right CCI path to follow, is to consider the degree of risk or innovation you are willing to undertake as a company. Safe CCI – for example supporting a well know charity or a very popular cause does not mean that it will be any less effective. However a corporation will need to be even more creative in its communications to make involvement in very mainstream CCI be in any way outstanding.

A sports sponsorship analogy might be of choosing to sponsor the Olympics, where the audience is big, but the event is so well sponsored and supported that the sponsors name risks disappearing unless the accompanying communications are very heavyweight and eye catching.

Alternatively, a company could sponsor a new up and coming sport, perhaps helping to create the events and beginning to be associated with the sport itself. The company then stands out more given the freshness of the sponsorship. However the risks are higher. What happens if the new sport does not catch on, if audiences turn away etc.

There is no right or wrong answer, but companies must consider the culture of their organisation and brands and then adopt a CCI scheme to match. We would expect innovative companies to support innovative CCI, family companies to help with family based CCI and so on. CCI should be true to your brand values in the same way that everything else you do as a business is.

What your marketing style says about you

There is some interesting research produced by the Future Foundation which looked at consumer perception of a range of well know companies, and asked for views on how they saw these companies in terms of being a good corporate citizen.

Typically it showed a clear correlation between a company's style of advertising and marketing and its perceived trustworthiness as a company. Therefore British Airways was seen as greedy and aggressive, yet Virgin was seen by 50 per cent as a 'good citizen'. Similarly Sky was rated very low in terms of good citizenship compared to the BBC which was seen as twice as credible as a good citizen. Other examples of companies in the same sector exhibiting very different ratings as good corporate citizens included Dixons which was one of the worst companies for corporate citizenship verses retail sector leaders such as The Body Shop, Marks and Spencer, Boots, Tesco, John Lewis and J Sainsbury.

In all cases those companies that had either aggressive advertising or had suffered bad PR experiences, all scored poorly in terms of being seen as companies to trust to be good corporate citizens.

The research did not cover other sectors that might be considered collectively un-trustworthy – for example it would be hard to imagine any one chemical company performing better in the trustworthiness stakes than another. Similarity, it would be surprising to see differences between car companies, or insurance companies – all areas where the public would have an overall view of a sector en mass, rather than being able to define one company's identity and character from another.

However, it is fascinating to see what an impact marketing style has on the perceived trustworthiness of a corporation, when it ought to have no impact whatsoever on the reality of the situation. Consumers took the view that a particularly aggressive or 'greedy' stance in advertising meant that the company advertising was more likely to be untrustworthy and therefore, by extension, the company itself was seen as not being so trustworthy or as being such a good corporate citizen in general terms.

Does any of this matter? The research would indicate it does. Consumers were then asked to describe their ideal company. The following attributes were given:

Adjective	Mentioned by
Honest	87 per cent
Fair	84 per cent
Trustworthy	77 per cent
Helpful	63 per cent
Innovative	48 per cent
Friendly	42 per cent

Companies whose advertising does not reinforce or reflect these areas of consumer interest may be appealing to the consumer's rational side – for example the side looking for a bargain, but the advertising will not be triggering the feelings shown above, which consumers are rating as very important in terms of building trust.

In summary, CCI efforts could be undermined if other areas of your communications are at odds in terms of style and tone. Are we likely to believe that a retailer, for example, is a good corporate citizen, if we experience their store displays and advertising as aggressive, price-led and constantly claiming excellent bargains?

How are we to feel if we encounter pushy sales staff or read about consumer dissatisfaction? None of these factors logically implies that this hypothetical retailer is a poor corporate citizen, or is not committed to CCI. However, the perception clouds whatever the reality may be.

We all tend to judge a briefing by its cover and those who are stewards of brands and corporate reputation should know this more acutely than most. The Chairman of SAS, the Scandinavian airline, once famously remarked that if there were dirty coffee stains on the pull down tables fixed to seat backs on aeroplanes, then people would think the engines were also poorly maintained, that safety was skimped on and that the airline offered poor service levels and value for money. All that from a single coffee stain.

His point was well made. Everything seen by the consumer says something about your brand and the best brands ensure that everything is consistent. If you wish to position yourself as aggressive in a market, this is fine if it helps win sales. However, do not try and then use CCI to enhance the business as it will be viewed as not credible and even as suspicious.

However, if you seriously seek to build a favourable profile through CCI, then remember that your other means of communication must be supportive of this tone.

Having considered these broad areas on whether CCI is going to be appropriate and if so, what role it will play and how overt it will be, you are now ready to begin detailed planning.

The Do Right Model for best practice CCI

chapter 5

Chapter 5:
The Do Right Model for best practice CCI

Where next?

This chapter contains the 'Do Right Model' – to help companies plot a route forward, taking into account their current situation and their aspirations.

This road map is based on newly conducted, in-depth research with major corporations and charities conducted for this publication. The research looked at best practice, prevailing viewpoints and the combined experience of these leading companies. I have also drawn on my own experience of advising numerous clients in this area for the last eight years.

The Blue Peter Principle

I am often asked what, in my opinion, is the best example of CCI. The most obvious answer is Tesco's Computers for Schools, which is undoubtedly a powerful role model.

However, there is one example of CCI which operates by far the most successful formula for any company looking to improve or develop its CCI. The ideal CCI campaign is the Blue Peter annual appeal.

The Blue Peter appeals are still going strong after many years and every year they manage to keep interest high without radically departing from the tried and trusted formula. It could be argued that they have the benefit of a fresh and enthusiastic audience which is constantly renewing itself with every generation and this makes the task easier – the need for innovation is less acute, perhaps.

However, the world of children's entertainment – like any market – changes and Blue Peter has had to evolve like all successful brands must. Relevance is as much an issue for the programme as for any product.

In case there are any readers who are not familiar with the typical Blue Peter appeal, this is briefly how it operates.

Every year, Blue Peter, which is a long running children's TV show on BBC1, organises an appeal. The theme for the year's appeal is announced by the programme – it could be to provide Land Rovers in Africa, or playground equipment for special needs schools.

Documentary style film is shown, portraying the issues faced by the affected groups of people. Normally the Blue Peter presenter will visit some relevant locations and interview some of the people who are suffering in some way to ask them how Blue Peter's help will make a difference. This produces emotive TV and clarifies the need, before urging viewers to help.

How viewers can help is then clearly explained. Normally it is a very simple task, such as collecting old stamps, drinks cans or foil, to be recycled and turned into cash.

A very clear target for the appeal is set – normally a sum of money, which equates to so many Land Rovers, items of play equipment, or whatever. Simple equations are made between what each item costs – e.g. one pound will buy food for a week.

Viewers can send in for fundraising packs, including posters, entry forms, ideas and tips on fundraising. Organised groups, such as the Scouts and Guides are mobilised to assist, as are schools. Normally there is a partner charity, which provides endorsement that the need is genuine and delivers reassurance that the money will be professionally deployed where it is needed.

Commercial sponsorship is secured, providing further distribution of the message – for example in retail outlets. The charity partner also promotes the appeal via its own communications network.

Every week, funds raised are reported back to the viewers, so everybody can see how near or far the appeal is from its target.

The appeal always has a clear end date. Once the appeal is over, the money is donated, thanks are given to the viewers and more film is shown of how the donated items are making life better for the recipients. It is very clear how the appeal funds – and the viewers – have made a difference to real people in need.

The reason why the Blue Peter appeals are successful, is that they include the 10 golden rules of successful CCI:

1.   Make a long term commitment
Consistent support of an idea and a format over many years.

2.   Don't skimp on communications
The programme provides a strong platform and there is dedication to communications, with simple messages – ie 'what is the issue? Here is how you can help, here are the results, thank you'.

3.   Keep it simple
Targets are clear and easily remembered and only one cause is supported at a time.

4. Make it easy to be involved

Viewer participation is made as easy as possible.

5. Get a charity partner

To administer and provide credibility.

6. Keep freshness and innovation alive

The appeal changes every year.

7. Be national and local

National appeal is underpinned by local support – eg posters, appeal packs, local media kits etc.

8. Support real need

The chosen charity identifies the appeal focus.

9. Support those causes your consumers care about

Viewer research shows areas of interest for the appeal.

10. Support causes that reflect your brand values

The need to help and care about those who are less fortunate is a core Blue Peter message.

While Blue Peter is very successful and its format is a very good role model, often the needs of business are more complex and greater limitations exist. The following model is designed to help companies who are looking to find the best CCI programme for their particular needs.

The Do Right Model

No two company's are the same, but the following road map is based on the collective views and experiences of leading companies and of experts in this field. Not only should it be a helpful planning guide for those new to this area, but it is also a useful benchmarking tool for existing CCI schemes and for those charged with running and keeping them fresh and relevant.

The Do Right Model, is a continuous planning and improvement tool, which is based on the inside out principle of management. Therefore, it is largely driven by an alignment of external stakeholder needs and internal requirements and resources. It is developed for use with outside audience groups, and looks at how their involvement can be included, rather than producing a CCI plan in isolation.

The Do Right Model for CCI

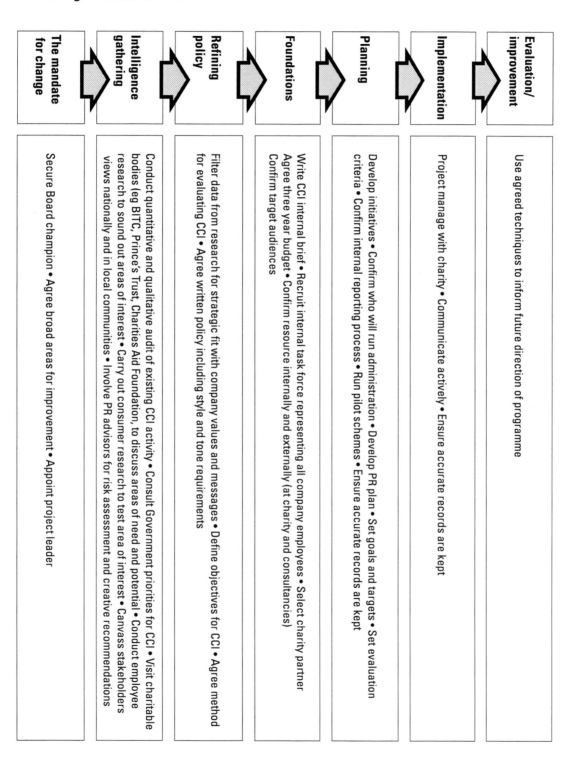

This seven stage model, will typically take five months to cover the planning and development stages. Evaluation is recommended after 12 months of implementation.

The seven stages in detail are as follows:

1. The mandate for change

All serious and radical change within a company must be supported at the highest level. The number of companies with a dedicated Corporate Citizenship Director is extremely rare, but at least one member of the Board must believe in the importance of CCI and champion this cause.

Fortunately the Chairman or Chief Executive are most usually aware of the reputational benefits of CCI and are often willing champions.

The other key player in the drive to improve CCI activity in terms of actual delivery, is most likely to be the Corporate Affairs Director, or someone with a similar external relations role. Depending on the nature of the CCI involved, it will be vital for this person to obtain the support of other relevant senior personnel – for example:

- Personnel/Human resources
- Marketing
- Government relations
- Community relations
- Local or area managers

Informal discussions at this level will be needed to sound out views on the current CCI activity and to explore broad feelings about how it might be improved.

If sufficient support in principle can be secured – a top line strategy paper should be sufficient to secure agreement to develop a fully researched plan

2. Intelligence gathering

The importance of this research phase is critical in order to:

- Assess the most appropriate CCI options
- Provide an opportunity for consultation in developing a blueprint for the future
- Establish and build relationships with key audiences
- Create a sense of perspective for what competitors and other leading companies are doing in this field

- Create a rational framework in which to judge the merits of existing CCI activities (rather than base decisions on personal preferences and old contacts).

The internal audit

Initially an internal audit of CCI activity should be completed. Typically this should be conducted via face to face meetings with a cross section of senior managers and employee representatives.

Some research should also be carried out with existing charity partners and others who currently are involved in the on going CCI activity.

An accurate picture of exactly what is being done, how much is being spent, how much given away etc, should be researched. This often proves far harder to ascertain than might be imagined. Often local branches will be supporting a plethora of local charities. Employees could be involved in a range of largely unrecorded activity. Donation of equipment or surplus/out of specification products are also often not recorded.

The audit should also canvas views on the value of existing activity and begin to explore views on areas for possible improvement.

Consultation with Government and the charitable and business community

Once the internal audit is completed there will be a clear picture of what needs to be changed and many views on how things might be improved.

The next stage is to begin looking outside for other stakeholder views. The Government is a good place to make the next stop on the roadmap. This is for two main reasons:

- Firstly, supporting Government backed schemes may well prove helpful in terms of future assistance from Government – eg attendance at launch events, advice from civil servants.

- Secondly, the Government will have clear ideas about where companies can get involved in issues and generally where that support would be most welcome.

Companies may prefer, rather than holding meetings, simply to review Government literature on the subject of good causes. A good quality political monitoring or Public Affairs company can help to provide a written summary of Government policy and areas of priority.

If face to face meetings are planned, it will be best to start with existing contacts. Alternatively, if a general area for support has been identified – eg health, or education, then that would clearly be the appropriate department to begin discussions.

Typically the relevant Ministerial advisors will be a good place to start the dialogue. Always attend these meetings with a clear idea of the information you need, your priorities and the

objectives you have for your CCI activity. With this information, the civil servant or politician will be able to provide a more appropriate matchmaking service.

In addition, companies may consider discussions with constituency MPs who cover their locations. Another route to cover is the relevant Minister or department which is most concerned with your business interest – this could be Consumer Affairs, Environment, The DTI or The Home Office, depending on the nature of your business and the issues you are looking to address through CCI.

Talk to the charitable sector

Organisations such as Business in the Community, The Charities Aid Foundation and The Prince's Trust can provide invaluable guidance on areas such as:

- Most needy areas for CCI

- Priorities with Government

- Areas which are already well supported (ie very competitive, with CCI saturation)

- Areas still to become 'owned' by any leading company

- Potential charity partners to consider

- Pros and cons of establishing a foundation or trust

- Likely costs for donations, administration, evaluation and PR support

- Options for evaluation

- Upcoming initiatives for support potential

- Access to consumer attitudinal research towards CCI

- Potential other business leaders to meet for further discussion.

Naturally these organisations will have specific areas of interest and they all have fundraising needs of their own. However, early consultation of this nature is likely to be offered at no charge.

Again, if a particular theme is beginning to emerge as a favourite, the company may wish to sit down with charities operating in this area, to begin to understand the issues, the options for CCI and the potential for partnership.

These discussions should remain informal. Generally it would not be advisable to ask charities to 'pitch' for your business. Although this does occur, charities often have limited resources and pitching can be an expensive and time intensive process. However, it is quite reasonable to ask a charity to discuss their credentials, the issues they are addressing and to consider how they might work with your company.

Listen to employees

Employee research is vital to identify causes that would be popular to support. However, it may be advisable to propose a number of themes and then test which would be most preferable. To canvass views entirely without boundaries, would lead to very diverse responses which would not be very helpful in terms of the decision making process. This is unless, of course, the company wants to set up a fund whereby employees can receive support for any cause. In which case, more open ended research will be helpful.

Employee research is also useful to identify any practical issues – eg large numbers of shift workers or temporary staff, long established links with local charities, or high levels of staff turnover, for example, all of which will affect the design of any CCI policy quite dramatically.

Consumer research

If consumers are a relevant audience, consumer research can be extremely useful to track views on:

- Current perceptions on your company as a corporate citizen

- Areas that are of concern where consumers feel your company should be doing more

- The type of CCI activity that consumers would prefer

- Preferred causes and charities

- Most favourably viewed CCI techniques – eg would they be motivated by CRM, a voucher collection scheme, recycling facilities, etc

- How and if consumers would like to hear about the CCI activity – should TV advertising be used, how about in store leaflets, etc

- What issues would change their view of the company if it supported social issues more

- How does the company compare to its competitors in the areas of being trustworthy and of being a good corporate citizen

- Your local community's expectations and priorities.

It may be interesting to note that MORI's consumer research showed the following issues to be ranked as the most important for large companies to support:

Q: How important do you think it is for large companies to contribute to or support the following?

Top 6 good causes	Percentage very/mainly important
The environment	86
Schemes for the unemployed	78
Job creation through small business	79
Crime prevention	72
Education	74
Help for disabilities	72

Source: MORI Corporate Social Responsibility Study
among British adults (August 1998)

National and local research

All research should be conducted both nationally and within local communities where the company operates – if appropriate. Views are likely to vary in a company's 'home turf' – both in terms of views about the corporation and about which issues matter most.

MORI's research of consumers shows that locally based good causes are some 20 per cent more popular than national causes.

Employees also tend to favour supporting local good causes. The ideal CCI campaign will accommodate the desire for localisation of activity, while using a high profile national theme to raise awareness.

Call in the PR team

A small but growing group of PR consultancies are now becoming experts in the field of CCI. PR companies are typically more sensitive to the wider issues and opportunities of companies supporting good causes. The Flora Diana margarine venture, which led to accusations of bad taste and which proved to be corporately embarrassing, was allegedly developed by a sales promotion team without the knowledge of the PR team.

It is not that sales promotion and advertising agencies are not highly useful in this area, it is simply that PR consultants should also be involved as they tend to be more sensitive to the potential pitfalls – as well as the areas for gain.

PR consultancies with relevant experience – and there are not that many who can claim to have such specialist knowledge – can be valuable partners at this research/audit stage:

- Third party independence brings a fresh pair of eyes and can also influence internal decisions more effectively than 'internal' recommendations

- The PR consultant which is experienced in this area, can offer views based on past work with other corporations looking to improve their CCI

- PR consultants will be able to draw on their (worst and best) experiences, to develop full risk management plans and crisis response procedures

- Finally, the PR consultant can draw upon the wider talents of the consultancy and develop creative CCI executions that will include PR-able activity as a built in feature. This is critical to ensure your CCI activity stands out among the competition

3. Refining policy

Commercial filtering

After the research phase, the company will essentially have a matrix showing what is happening now, what can be changed, where each stakeholder group would like to see new effort, and possible partners for the journey ahead.

The output from the matrix needs now to be filtered via cross reference with the company's values and key messages. If the good cause themes and activities recommended by the research sit well with company messages, then it is evident that supporting these themes will enhance the corporate reputation and reinforce desired messages being delivered via other communication routes.

The task is to whittle down options thrown up by the research to include only those that fit strategically with the business goals. Aligning the various needs of all the stakeholders is the ultimate task.

A CCI policy that meets the approval of as many audiences as possible will be one that is built to last.

This view of CCI could be interpreted as cynical. Only adopting initiatives and causes that are both popular and which support commercial goals is not the true spirit of CCI.

For a minority of companies, CCI is indeed not run in this way. Some will simply choose to support causes because they believe in them – this support may then be completely invisible in terms of promotional activity. Others will promote their support of the issue, but the commercial gain is secondary to the desire to publicise the issues and to campaign for change.

However, research for this briefing, shows that the vast majority of companies – even those with highly sophisticated approaches to CCI and with long term track records of commitment to communities – will seek to support themes that are relevant to their business interests.

It is not that these companies ignore the wider issues, the areas of real need or more minority areas worthy of CCI support. It is more that they look for common ground and win win areas, where every stakeholder audience feels served.

It seems to me to be completely unreasonable to expect companies to allocate their shareholders money for CCI activity in any direction other than that which is supportive or reflective of their business interests. To suggest that companies should instead totally follow the agendas of consumers or the government is unrealistic. Clearly companies will benefit from getting balance between self interest and wider concerns, however, companies will ultimately always seek to secure CCI schemes based on enlightened self interest.

Defining objectives

The person in charge of the process, will now be in a position to develop objectives for the new CCI activities. This simple set of statements is very often omitted and with all activity, a lack of objectives will often lead to a difficulty in measurement and evaluation, a lack of shared expectations and therefore disappointment.

Objectives should be as specific as possible and consider areas such as:

- The role of the CCI
- Who it should reach
- Where it should operate
- The affect it should have
- The benefits it should bring.

Evaluation

The objectives set should be measurable. Therefore, it is always a good discipline to write the measurement criteria at the same time as the objectives. Therefore if the CCI is designed to improve the reputation of the business, it must be clear with whom the reputation should

be improved, by how much and for what reasons – eg the objective might be: raise awareness among factory employees of the scale of the company's CCI by 10 per cent.

Once the objectives have been developed in this way, it will be necessary to consider how each objective will be tracked. In the example above, employee research before and after would be the answer. Another form of evaluation might be to set up small panels from each target audience group and ask them to report back every 4 months – not as rigorous as full scale research, but it could be an answer if budgets are tight.

Other targets or milestones should also be considered at this stage as regards the performance of the CCI itself – eg to provide a family holiday for 400 disadvantaged children over the next three years, or to provide 500 hours of voluntary support over the next 12 months.

For this type of evaluation, it will be essential to work with your charity partner, HR Director and others to ensure adequate record keeping processes for CCI exist. The amount of CCI activity that is only ever recorded through anecdote is still very high in even the largest and most sophisticated company.

CCI Policy

The messages, objectives and methods of evaluation all form the basis of the CCI Policy Statement. This document should set out:

- The issues to be address by the CCI activity

- The desired messages the CCI activity should convey

- The objectives of CCI activity

- The strategic route forward to achieve those objectives

- The ways in which the objectives will be measured

- The obstacles – if any, that must be overcome

- The target audiences for the CCI

- Key areas of focus – eg from the company view: employee motivation, consumer loyalty, political support etc; plus the focus in terms of good causes: support for families, the disabled, inner city crime prevention, homelessness etc

- Desired style and tone of the CCI – eg should it be conventional, radical, surprising, mainstream etc (this should be reflective of the company's style and values)

- Any key dos and don'ts – eg areas that will not be supported, attitudes to national and local activity, will there be a single focus or several? How much autonomy will there be for local divisions of the company, or for individual employees?

This document is vital in that it provides a strategic framework for the CCI activity, and creates a rational, well researched way forward.

4. Foundations

With the broad policy signed off, the detailed planning can now begin. The CCI policy statement should now form the basis of a specific brief or set of briefs from which one or more CCI initiatives will be developed.

Each campaign within the CCI programme should have its own brief. This should include all the key elements to be found within any creative brief, namely:

- Target audiences
- Key messages
- Areas for focus of good cause
- Measurable objectives
- Desired areas for CCI to support
- Resource available
- Timescale involved (three year planning is recommended)
- Reasons for wanting to do CCI
- How the CCI should be communicated
- Key people involved in delivering the CCI initiative.

The brief is a very important document which will be given to charity partners to help them develop specific campaigns to support the CCI activities.

The brief can also be used internally, to ask individual teams or company locations how they would respond with their own initiatives to support the overall goals.

Charity partners

The key rules for gaining the best out of your relationship with your charity partners are very simple. Research for this briefing shows that the most important things to establish are the following:

- Remember that a charity will not always have the level of resource you might be used to in the commercial world. A company should seriously consider helping to provide an element of funding to ensure there is sufficient administrative support on a day to day basis for the CCI partnership.

- An honest and open relationship is essential. Time and time again it proves increasingly beneficial if time is invested in integrating the charity contacts into as much of the CCI decision making process and thinking as possible.

- Regular on going contact once the CCI scheme is up and running is vital. The company should allocate a day to day contact who can liaise with the charity on a regular basis.

- For areas such as design, PR and marketing support, companies may do well to ensure their own designers, PR and marketing teams are involved at an early stage, to ensure that professional communication standards are obtained, in a style that you would expect for all other areas of your business.

- Remember to say thank you – charity teams are human too and will welcome any feedback and involvement in the debates that take place around CCI activity. Like any relationship, the one between company and charity, needs working at and a significant time investment will be required to ensure expectations are aligned, and an agreed level of service is delivered to each party

Choosing the right charity, will of course depend on the cause area being supported. Views can be taken from independent bodies like Business in the Community or the Charities Aid Foundation, and of course, chemistry/credentials meetings need to be held with 3 or 4 charities to discuss potential partnerships. However, making charities pitch formally is not recommended, as discussed before, due to the unacceptable burden this puts on their scarce resources.

Budget allocation

Naturally, budgets will vary dramatically according to the scope of the CCI involved. However, I have prepared the following guidelines, based on the research carried out for this briefing and on the experience of many major corporations, plus the advice of CCI intermediaries.

I have outlined a fairly typical CCI programme and indicated typical costs and the percentage of each cost, so that a company may put its own figures into this model. Clearly this is just one example, but it is based on extensive research of leading companies in the CCI area, so should be seen as fairly typical.

The example below shows a fairly typical CCI initiative that is targeting employees, and opinion formers only.

Activity	Estimated annual cost	Percentage of total
Core funding donation to charity (to help run CCI programme)	10,000	4
Donation to good cause itself – eg via grants	150,000	67
Evaluation	10,000	5
Production of supporting literature, information materials, posters etc	15,000	7
PR support and other communications needs – eg photography, press packs, speeches, local guidelines, crisis and issues plan	20,000	9
Administration budget – travel, secretarial support	10,000	4
Event support – eg launch events, cheque presentations, local events	10,000	4
Total	**225,000**	**100**

Where there is a need to communicate to the general public and to a very high level of employees – eg to all branches of a national retailer, the costs involved will be considerably higher, in terms of the level of donation, administration and advertising/PR.

The possible scale and range of scales is so great in these cases, that it seems impractical to suggest typical budgets. However, the basic components shown above will still all be required. The proportions of spend should largely remain the same, although the elements related to communications and to support material, could as much as double in terms of percentage, given the dramatically larger audiences involved.

Risk management and crisis planning

The final element in the Foundations stage, is to put a very black hat on and envisage every possible scenario which could be negative and damaging. Fraud, injury during volunteering schemes, charity criticisms, accusations of exploitation - these are just a few of the issues that could arise.

Detailed risk management plans are needed for the most severe risks, including risk avoidance plans and contingency plans should issues arise.

Detailed Q&As should be developed, so there is clarity and consistency in answers given as to why the CCI scheme is being run, how it is managed and so on.

This area is well suited to the skills of the PR consultant, who will draft these materials in conjunction with people from around the business. It is definitely worth involving a range of company representatives in this process. For example, there could be local issues about supporting local vs national charities, or surrounding employee dissatisfaction at CCI donations, if there have been cuts in areas such as staffing, for example.

The key to risk management is envisaging every possible scenario - no matter how ugly or unlikely - and then considering how the company can avoid these issues occurring in the first place and also how it would respond if these events did take place.

The charity partner should also share in this process as they may be aware of other issues not apparent to the company, and they may also find themselves in the front line of difficult questions and therefore must be able to respond.

Finally, it is essential to involve your legal advisors during the planning stage of your CCI as part of the crisis and issues management process. CRM schemes, for example, will almost always require a legal undertaking between the corporation and the charitable partner. The same will apply for a media partnership. Legal advice should be sought on liability, periods of termination between company and charity, contingency for fraud, insurance and every other eventuality that your legal team can consider.

It would be unfair to suggest that CCI is an area which is particularly prone to litigation. However, it is prudent to ask your advisors to cast their eyes over plans to look for legal pitfalls and to include any necessary precautions through the contract or letter of agreement.

5. Planning

Designing the CCI activities is now the key task within the next stage of the Do Right model - ie what the initiative should be and how it should be run.

Choosing which initiatives to support and how they are executed, should be the product of a meeting of a group of informed individuals, typically including the following:

- Corporate Community Director, or equivalent senior management leader
- PR advisor plus advertising/sales promotion teams if appropriate
- Charity partner

- HR Director

- Local community relations manager (if relevant)

This group should work on detailed plans for final sign off by the Board level champion – ideally at Chairman or Chief Executive level.

The research work to date, internal discussion and creative ideas, will provide the basis for deciding on what the chosen CCI schemes should be like in practice.

However, there may be other factors, such as desired target audiences to be reached, the favourability and trustworthiness of the sector, current position, track record and so on, which will also influence the type of CCI that is going to be most effective.

The summary chart below provides guidance for the do right company, in terms of the type of CCI which might suit individual circumstances. This planning tool is designed to help companies develop CCI which is reflective of their needs, their current status and their aspirations for the future.

Level of profile (awareness and favorability) — Low to High

CCI tactics	Poor reputation for sector	Poor reputation for company	Need to unite employees and build morale	New business	Need to reach political/opinion former audience	Limited internal resource dedicated to CCI	Employees and customers all over UK	Mature business	Reputation for cutting edge style	High profile brand	Need to boost consumer sales
Philanthropy	✓	✓	✗	✓	✗	✗	✓	✓	✗	✗	✗
Donation of equipment	✓	✗	✓	✗	✗	✗	✗	✓	✗	✗	✗
Donation of time/pro bono work	✓	✗	✓	✓	✗	✗	✓	✓	✓	✗	✗
Employee volunteering	✓	✗	✓	✓	✗	✗	✓	✓	✓	✓	✗
Employee mentoring	✓	✓	✓	✓	✗	✗	✓	✓	✓	✓	✗
Employment opportunities for disadvantaged	✓	✓	✓	✗	✗	✓	✓	✓	✓	✓	✗
Bridging causes and supporters	✗	✓	✗	✗	✓	✗	✓	✗	✓	✓	✗
Seedcorn funding	✓	✗	✗	✗	✓	✓	✗	✗	✗	✗	✗
Grant distribution	✗	✗	✗	✗	✓	✓	✓	✗	✓	✗	✗
Supporting small charity	✗	✗	✗	✓	✓	✓	✗	✗	✓	✗	✗
Operate local CCI	✓	✗	✓	✗	✓	✓	✓	✓	✓	✓	✓
Mass employee involvement	✗	✗	✓	✓	✗	✗	✓	✓	✓	✓	✓
Support bigger/higher profile charity	✗	✗	✓	✗	✗	✗	✓	✓	✗	✓	✓
Operate national/international CCI	✗	✗	✓	✗	✗	✗	✓	✓	✗	✓	✓
Provide platform for issues	✗	✗	✗	✓	✗	✗	✗	✓	✓	✗	✗
Cause related marketing	✗	✗	✗	✗	✗	✗	✓	✓	✓	✓	✓
Fair trade	✗	✗	✗	✓	✓	✗	✓	✓	✓	✗	✓

Piloting CCI schemes

Before the CCI initiative chosen is fully rolled out, it is always advisable to run a few pilot versions, either limited by scale, geographic region or with 'home' audiences- eg employees and local communities only.

This can provide very valuable learning to avoid pitfalls later on. It is also a useful consultation exercise and demonstrates a robust approach to CCI development that will be impressive internally as well as to external opinion formers.

6. Implementation

The four essentials during implementation of CCI

Of course there will be endless activities required to make the CCI run smoothly. However, research carried out specially for this briefing has indicated three main areas which need to be ensured, if the CCI programme is to deliver against its objectives, and if it is to deliver value to the corporation:

- **The devil is in the admin**. Ensure there is sufficient resource in the company and at the charitable partners to project manage the administration of the CCI scheme adequately. All too often this aspect is overlooked and insufficient resources are provided.

- **Communicate, communicate and communicate**. Internal reporting, links with charities and good causes, employee communications dialogue with communities, the media, other parts of the business and opinion former groups, are all essential to build enthusiasm and support.

  Ensure that sufficient resources and platforms are in place to deliver regular communications to all stakeholders. This is one of the most frequently mentioned areas of concern from large companies. Again it requires considerable resource and creativity to ensure the communications are engaging and deliver the required messages.

- **Keep accurate records**. Make it easy to record CCI activity. Credit is so often lost when in fact it is due.

- **Keep checking the road map**. Cross checking back to your objectives will keep things on the right track. If you know where you want to be, you will know if you are getting there.

7. Evaluation

Evaluation and measurement should always be based on the original objectives and include targets for improvement. Evaluation should always be viewed as a dynamic tool for forward planning rather than an end of project justification exercise.

Summary checklist for do right companies

Developing CCI schemes takes a lot of research and detailed work. Hopefully the Do Right Model will provide busy managers with some assistance on this journey.

The key points exhibited by leading corporations who have achieved do right company status – as revealed in research for this briefing – are simple guidelines that we can all follow:

- Keep things simple
- Get a good charity partner
- Make sure there is enough resource set aside for administration and project management
- Make sure your CCI is eye catching and is capable of involving all target audiences in a way that will generate PR interest
- Dedicate enough resource to PR and communications in general
- Set measurable objectives – know what you want to achieve from CCI
- Agree evaluation methods at the beginning
- Get senior level buy in
- Choose a theme and stick to it
- Choose interesting causes and make them come alive locally

Above all, remember you are not alone. CCI is one area where people are willing to offer advice and inspiration to those businesses and brands looking to become do right companies.

CCI is useful for the business in itself, but the process of developing a CCI policy and of joining this world, brings relationship building opportunities along the way.

Discussion centred on CCI can bring a company into contact with politicians, the media, employee representatives and business peers in a way that promotes the company's reputation in a positive way. In this sense, the process of developing a CCI programme presents a very useful platform for relationship building at all levels.

In the course of researching this briefing, leading multi-national business managers were asked what would be the single most important piece of advice they would give to another business looking to set up a CCI programme. The most frequently cited comments were as follows:

> *'Don't re-invent the wheel – there are a lot of people who have done this sort of thing before and they can be very helpful in providing guidance'*

> *'Clear objectives are vital'*

> *'Always ask yourself – will it make a difference?'*

> *'Do research'*

> *'Make sure your CCI fits with the company culture'*

> *'Choose a theme and stick to it'*

> *'Secure senior management support – you will need it to get the resources that will be necessary'*

Good advice for companies wishing to follow the Do Right Model.

International CCI roll out

CCI is well established in the USA, Canada, South Africa, Japan, Germany and many parts of Asia, and South America. However, it is not commonly seen in many European countries, although specific examples do exist.

Nevertheless, many multi-national corporations are rolling out CCI programmes in all markets as a way of building a unified feel across the globe and as a core part of how they do business in a market.

Managers operating CCI on a global basis, should consider developing templates giving guidance, suggested themes, policies and a range of suggested ways forward, backed up by case studies of good practice from other countries which might act as inspiration.

Local managers can then adapt the centrally generated plan for local implementation.

A clear and regular reporting procedure so the centre can monitor activity, investment and results is crucial.

The manager with this responsibility, will undoubtedly need to spend time visiting markets, encouraging local participation, celebrating success, gathering examples of good practice, trouble shooting and generally spreading the good word around the globalised operation.

More and more companies are operating in this way, achieving economies of scale, more control and a greater understanding of what is happening around the world, plus ever higher standards of CCI, thanks to better sharing of information and experience.

My research shows that the most effective scenario is one where very clear guidelines are issued from the centre at a policy level, but where local companies then have a reasonable amount of freedom to develop and implement their own schemes.

There are very few CCI programmes that are directed or implemented centrally on a global basis. The familiar mantra of 'Think global, act local', seems to be the preferred style of the blue chip multi-nationals that participated in the research for this publication.

Communications

chapter 6

Chapter 6:
Communications

'Therefore when thou doest thine alms, do not sound a trumpet before thee, as the hypocrites do in the synagogues and in the streets, that they may have glory of men. But when thou doest alms, let not thy left hand know what thy right hand doeth.'

Matthew chapter 6

Shaking the collection bag

As a consultant advising companies on their CCI, the area which I am asked about most frequently and which seems to cause the most anguish and frustration, is the communication of CCI.

Or to be more specific, the issue of how to gain recognition for the corporation's support of good causes. Often, managers feel disappointed that the genuinely significant investment on supporting charitable causes or community initiatives is not more widely known.

This feeling can be acutely felt when a company comes under attack in the media for a particular issue. When faced with such criticism, company executives become aware of how little people know about all the good they do in society. Instead, the media focuses on the bad news and any positive CCI is lost in the sensationalism of the negative story.

Many managers feel that if the good works their corporations performed in society were more widely understood, then the media, consumer groups, green groups and other pressure organisations, would be more sympathetic.

Personally, I think that a company's track record in helping with social issues, can improve the reputation of that company and that this will provide a goodwill force field that can protect the company to some extent if other areas of the business come under fire.

Virgin Trains have been highly criticised, but the overall reputation of Virgin and its founder Richard Branson have remained intact. This is because Virgin is seen as a good corporate citizen generally, and occasional lapses are more tolerated.

M&S, similarly tarnished in terms of reputation, will I am sure regain the trust of the public and the media more rapidly (assuming they get the business working well again, of course) than another company might experience, because they have greater reputation collateral, following years of outstanding, trust building performance.

However, it would be naive to assume that every company could protect or rebuild its reputation in this way through better awareness of its CCI. Sometimes, the perception of the business is too negative to be neutralised by CCI. It is hard to imagine a tobacco company winning favour through CCI, no matter how major their donations. Other specific companies and entire sectors are faced with consumer hostility that runs too deep for CCI alone to rectify.

In fact, when a company faces such deep seated reputation issues, CCI may be entirely inappropriate – or at least high profile types of corporate citizenship. The prejudices that such companies face, mean that everything they do is treated with suspicion and the CCI is interpreted as guilt money. The company is seen to be using its profits to win over the hearts and minds of politicians and the public through the cynical exploitation of attractive charitable causes. In these cases, the CCI is seen as a distracting perfume to cover up the stench of the company's misdemeanours.

This backlash against the CCI activity simply draws more attention to the reputation issues faced by the business – perpetuating rather than addressing the problem.

This does not mean that no CCI is the answer. CCI can be very helpful for companies faced with media or pressure group hostility. CCI can help keep employee morale up and can provide useful material for discussion with opinion formers. However, in such cases, low profile activity aimed at internal and opinion former audiences only, would be most appropriate.

Fortunately most managers do not find themselves operating in such a combative environment. So the question still remains, how can I make the company's CCI better known and appreciated?

The big issue

In the research of managers responsible for CCI carried out for this briefing, publicising CCI was clearly a hot issue.

71 per cent said that publicity potential was either extremely important, or one of the most important areas to be considered, when deciding on what community initiatives to support.

None of the respondents were planning to spend less over the next 12 months on publicising their good works: 70 per cent said they would be spending about the same and the remainder claimed they would be spending more. The amount currently being spent as a percentage of the total CCI spend varied form 0.5 per cent to 20 per cent, with the average being 5.4 per cent of the total CCI budget.

Traditionally there has been reticence about publicising a company's CCI. Concerns about appearing to be making reputational mileage out of other people's misfortune was one issue, along with fears about a media backlash and a general sense that it was inappropriate to boast in this area – the corporate equivalent to shaking the collection bag in church so everyone hears your money being donated.

This feeling of reluctance was still evident with some of the companies I interviewed and who completed my questionnaire. However, in most cases, these comments came from companies that have had precarious reputation issues in the past and who have been burned by the media once too often to risk high profile attempts to promote themselves as a good corporate citizen.

By and large, the majority of companies are very comfortable with promoting their CCI as widely as possible, and in fact would like to do even more to get their activities known.

Only 17 per cent of those surveyed felt that companies should not be seen to be publicising any good works, apart from to discrete groups that need to know in order to get involved – eg charities or local community leaders. The remaining 83 per cent agreed with the view that companies should publicises their support of good causes as widely as possible to all relevant audiences.

The commercial drive for accountability in every area of modern business life and the competitive pressures to win the trust of the public for a corporation or a brand, has led to most managers loosing any reticence they may have had for publicising CCI as hard and aggressively as they promote other areas of the business.

The prize of developing a reputation for good corporate citizenship into a competitive edge is well worth the investment required in communicating a business's CCI activity.

Companies that achieve the charmed status of being trusted as good corporate citizens become what I describe as 'reputation snowballs'. They are essentially well thought of and as a result consumers believe they are trustworthy in every area of their business – even when there is no evidence or experience to substantiate this view. Their good reputation builds on itself like a snowball, long after the original reason for liking the company is gone. One consequence of this is that the most routine announcement of a business's development is reported in the media and portrayed as another example of corporate excellence.

A similar announcement for a mainstream competitor that is a good company, but which does not enjoy the 'reputation snowball' status, would gain no mention in the media. Conversely, the opposite applies to companies who start off with a poor reputation in terms of trustworthiness. At the extreme end, this means that virtually everything that company does – no matter how innocuous – is turned into a negative exemplar of the business's shortcomings.

CHAPTER 6: COMMUNICATIONS

So it is clear to see why company managers are keen to build a reputation for being a good corporate citizen. The urge to promote CCI activity is entirely appropriate according to the public and other audiences, who appear to expect companies to communicate their support of social issues. MORI's definitive research into the area of CCI, shows 72 per cent of consumers agree with the view that companies should communicate about their CCI, but that they should not spend significant amounts of money in the process.

Only 17 per cent felt it was acceptable to spend heavily on communications, although one would imagine that the public would take this view on the appropriateness of spending on communications for any issue. Just 8 per cent felt that promotion of CCI was not important and therefore no money should be spent on it.

The public appear to be accepting of the view that companies will embark on CCI activity for commercial gain – MORI's poll shows 61 per cent of consumers believing that it is acceptable for companies to derive some benefit from CCI.

What works and what doesn't

In the new research carried out for this briefing, managers responsible for CCI in major corporations were asked which promotional methods they used to publicise their community involvement, and which audiences they targeted.

MORI's survey of consumers asked them to rank which methods of communications were appropriate for companies to use to communicate CCI and – for those that were aware of initiatives – MORI asked how they found out about them.

Below I have, combined MORI's data with information from research for this briefing, to provide views of the public and the views of the professional CCI manager, side by side:

Promotional methods	Promotional methods used by business (%)	Q: Companies who actively support the community can communicate their activities in different ways. Which do you feel are the most appropriate? (MORI)	Promotional methods disliked by public (%)	Q: How did you find out about their social or community activities? (MORI)
TV advertising	3	46	17	11
Press advertising	6	36	12	13
Stories on local TV/press	N/A	38	6	16
Stories on national TV/press	N/A	29	7	9
All PR/media relations	28	N/A	N/A	N/A
Leaflets in store	N/A	31	13	14
Charity scheme/event	17	26	5	13
Website	N/A	16	23	0
Community activity report	25	11	5	1

It should be stressed that the survey for this briefing and the MORI survey were carried out completely separately. The same questions were not used in both surveys – hence the N/As shown above. While I would not claim that the two sets of data are comparable in any meaningful way. I have presented them together for ease of comparison.

Most notably, we see two key points:

- the importance of advertising for the consumer – not typically used to promote CCI

- The importance of media relations in promoting CCI via editorial coverage. This is a clear area where there is common ground between the managers and the consumer

Additional publicity activities listed in my research were: face to face presentations for opinion formers and the public, newsletters for employees, and client entertaining. The first two of these activities were very popular and used by around 20 per cent of respondents

How successful is CCI PR?

Respondents reported targeting a wide range of audiences in the research for this briefing:

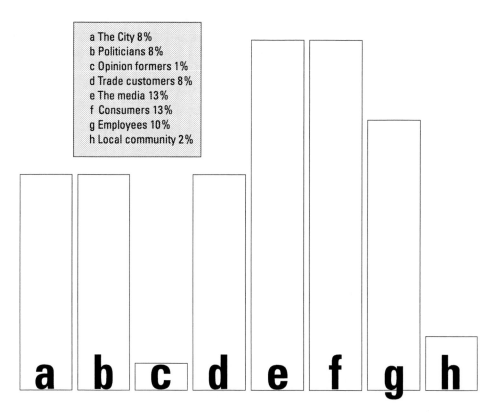

a The City 8%
b Politicians 8%
c Opinion formers 1%
d Trade customers 8%
e The media 13%
f Consumers 13%
g Employees 10%
h Local community 2%

Source: author's research (Dec-Jan 98/9)

When asked to what extent they felt that they were being successful in achieving recognition for their corporation's CCI according to each audience, the following results were produced:

Audience	Well recognised	Adequately recognised	Virtually unrecognised	Not relevant
The City	2	4	4	2
Politicians	1	6	5	0
Opinion formers	0	6	6	0
Trade customers	0	6	5	0
The media	2	4	6	0
Consumers	0	8	14	1
Employees	5	6	1	0
Local community	3	7	2	0

What this tends to indicate is a polarised view between companies either feeling that they are performing well or not in the case of most audiences – this shows that many managers feel this area of communication is one still needing attention.

However, what is most interesting to note is the overwhelming success with employees and the local community and – by contrast – the lack of success with the consumer in terms of communicating CCI.

The thought that the consumer is the most difficult nut to crack, was reinforced during the in depth qualitative interviews carried out for this briefing with senior managers of major corporations. Many have chosen not to focus on reaching this group, given the lack of success to date.

Respondents in the self completion questionnaire issued for this briefing, were asked what they felt were the main obstacles that needed to be overcome to achieve consumer recognition for good corporate citizenship. The most frequently cited factor was cynicism and suspicion of business in this area.

When asked if they ever felt that awareness of CCI activity among the public would ever improve, most were optimistic: 46 per cent felt that things would improve within five years, another 46 percent felt it would take between five and 15 years.

This prognosis of slow progress in terms of consumer awareness, is confirmed by MORI which reports virtually no increase in consumer awareness of specific CCI initiatives year on year.

The public's scepticism continues to be fuelled by the media and pressure groups. Business does not have a strong champion in the area of CCI to help redress the balance by telling society about the contribution businesses make to social and community concerns.

The two generic business organisations – the Institute of Directors and the Confederation of British Industry perform excellently in terms of promoting business in general economic terms, but they seem to cover the area of corporate citizenship very rarely.

The principle promoter of business involvement in good causes is BITC. Their work with the *Financial Times* and elsewhere to promote business's involvement in CCI is admirable. However, BITC's main role is to encourage business involvement, not to promote that involvement to the public. I for one would like to see a body set up to promote – at a generic level and to a wide audience – the contributions made by business to the community.

There is also no clear champion for CCI at Government level. We often hear ministers talking about how they will be keeping business in check, but there is very little high profile celebration by politicians of the contribution business makes to social costs through CCI.

Clearly there may well be reticence to highlight the part played by business in funding areas that should arguably be provided by the Government – school books, computers for schools, and so on. However, the public has indicated that it understands and expects business to play its part in helping to tackle social needs. Perhaps the consumer backlash that politicians seem to fear, might not be such an issue after all.

Building the perfect CCI PR machine

Creating PR-able elements within a CCI programme of activities needs to be done at the planning stage for maximum benefit. PR should be built in at the design stage as it will then be evident how and when the CCI can be promoted right from the outset.

All too often, the CCI activity is agreed, runs for a while and then an attempt is made to publicise the activity. This is rarely effective, as the CCI will not necessarily have been developed to deliver any newsworthy material.

In talking about PR in relation to CCI, I am including all aspects of communications including advertising, literature production, point of sale material and so on.

Of course, creating a PR programme for a CCI activity is no different to building a PR campaign for anything else. The same rules and principles apply. There are no special conditions just because the subject matter is a good cause. The media will not show any favouritism nor will any other target audience.

As with all communications, the task for the CCI manager is to convey features of the CCI and benefits for each target audience. Information must convey the rational side of the CCI scheme as well as the emotional.

There are two main areas of difficulty when communicating CCI externally:

1. The national media (newspapers, TV, radio and the women's press) are typically not interested in reporting positive CCI stories

2. It is therefore difficult to reach consumers via this route.

Any experienced PR company will be able to develop a programme of activity to reach all audiences. However, the following points will be helpful for managers who are looking to obtain the maximum impact in terms of promoting their company's CCI.

Branding

Like anything in communications, it will help to stimulate interest in a CCI campaign if the initiative can be well branded. Companies should consider developing a creative name and strapline for the activity – eg *'Quit – the xyz company's campaign to stub out under age smoking.'*

A campaign logo should also be considered, perhaps incorporating the company logo. This can be used on literature, signage, special press release paper, giant cheques, on vehicles, and merchandise items.

Events

Typically, the company should consider a launch event for the CCI campaign. This could be for opinion formers, with a relevant politician as the guest speaker. The event could be held at a newsworthy venue – eg at a school or a community centre where the good cause will be implemented.

As well as a national event, regional events can be useful – ideally involving local employees and MPs. These events can become annual after the launch, as they can be used to announce progress and to announce the next phase of CCI.

Stretching the story

When issuing press material, it is worth trying to maximise the number of reasons to make a press statement over the year. For example, if the CCI involves local charities applying for help, the first release could be the appeal to local charities/schools etc to get involved. This can be followed by a subsequent release announcing the local charities/ schools etc that have been successful. The next story opportunity is when the money is handed over. Another story is created when the project supported by the donation is complete.

This simple technique of planning the unfolding story in stages will help to increase the number of occasions the story is covered.

A press relations template is also often useful, so local offices can develop their own regional media information, based on centrally created guidelines.

Case studies

Depending on the nature of the CCI, there may be a media opportunity to create written case studies on the projects that have been assisted. Journalists could visit selected schemes. Alternatively, another successful technique is to arrange for a local school or MP to visit one of the charitable schemes. This will create more media interest and a better accompanying photograph.

Regionality

If a CCI activity can be broken down so that it is supporting local causes (even if they are national themes or charities involved), then the opportunity for local and regional media coverage will be dramatically increased. Local and regional media are only interested in any story that is taking place in their area. Your CCI needs to be able to provide local interest stories, if you wish to secure media coverage of this kind.

National politicians

Relevant Ministers should always be invited to attend key events, such as the annual launch event.

In addition, companies should aim to organise a face to face briefing of Ministers or their advisors if the CCI activity is significant.

Local MPs

Constituency MPs should be invited to local events such as cheque handovers, visits to good causes, and major announcements. Always organise any media activity with constituency MPs on a Friday as they will typically be in their constituencies on this day.

Think pictures

Always consider the visual aspect of any story. Involving children, animals, celebrities or interesting aspects of the CCI, will all help bring the story to life for both print and broadcast media. Always have sufficient branded signage or other materials available for use in pictures

Local employees

The usual methods of communication with employees can carry the CCI story - staff newsletters, intranet sites, notice boards etc should all be targeted. However, more innovative techniques can be considered to involve employees - eg special themed days when displays related to

the CCI theme are put up around the building, or when everyone wears a button badge. Special videos can be created and existing events – such as company conferences – should always include references to the CCI work and how people can get involved.

Typically, the best results will occur if internal promotional activity is concentrated over a relatively short period of time. Local employees should also be used in the regional media wherever possible – perhaps visiting a project that has received assistance or welcoming visitors from the charity to the company's local offices/shop or factory.

Media partners

Obtaining editorial coverage in the national media (apart from in specialist business or charitable community publications) is extremely unlikely given the nature of most CCI. One option to obtain national media coverage is to develop the CCI in partnership with a media group. The merits and issues of this have been discussed already, but it does provide a guaranteed way of securing interest in national publications – something that otherwise is unlikely to be available.

Related advertisements, competitions and sales promotions

Other controlled ways of communicating the messages concerning your CCI activity include traditional advertising, which is a technique used quite extensively in the opinion former media, but less well used in mainstream consumer media. The notable exception to this being BT which advertises its CCI involvement very heavily on national TV and in national print media.

In addition to advertising, managers could consider the use of competitions in the media that relate to the cause being supported – eg if your business's CCI activity was to help the RSPCA, then you might run editorial competitions which offer wildlife holidays, or wildlife videos and books as prizes. The competition copy should then be designed to raise awareness of the company's CCI support and of the importance of the issue in question.

Direct mailshots can also be developed to raise awareness of the CCI. These could be existing mailers – eg bills, or details of new products, which can carry the CCI message – even involving a cause related element if relevant – eg, if you buy this product, we will donate 'x' amount to the following cause which we have been supporting for so many years etc etc.

Commenting on the cause

Not every company may wish to give comments on the cause which their CCI activity is looking to address. However, for those that do feel comfortable, issuing media statements and getting involved in the debate around the issues, can help raise the corporation's profile.

There needs to be a highly informed and articulate spokesperson who is willing to talk on behalf of the company. This is rarely a reasonable role for any employee within the vast majority of companies.

To date, relatively few companies have taken a visible position on issues that they are helping to address. The exceptions primarily being ethically driven companies like The Body Shop or the Co-op.

Creative mailings

Companies could consider mail shots to journalists or opinion formers that highlight the good causes they support and which then show how the company is supporting that cause.

To avoid accusations of profligacy, these mailings should always have a double purpose – not simply be pieces of promotional material. For example, they could also be invitations to an event, or be attached to a press release. For similar reasons of taste, the mailings should not appear to have expensive production values.

Formal literature

It is worth compiling an annual report or some single piece of literature (perhaps with an accompanying video) that lays out the company's CCI activities, its policies and values.

By making this an annual publication, it is possible to update the information and include new case studies and progress made against targets. The annual report also offers the opportunity for the company to track its impact in CCI with a similar rigour as that which is seen with financial results.

The literature item can also provide application details for those good causes looking to get involved or looking for support. This single piece of communication can be distributed at events, mailed to the media or opinion formers and used with employees and at other face to face briefings.

Popular materials

For mass communications to either staff or to consumers in high street locations or in their homes via mailings, it is necessary to have a range of lower cost, consumer friendly items of literature to get the CCI message across.

Many companies surveyed for this briefing produce in-store leaflets, posters, carrier bags and point of sale display items to communicate their CCI activity. In every case, these were in addition to the more formal documents described above, which were aimed more at opinion formers.

High volume lower cost materials are also useful for distribution to employees, where numbers involved can be very high.

Speaker platforms/business networking

Senior managers should seek out conference opportunities to present details of their CCI to business peers as this helps to develop a reputation as a leading proponent of CCI.

Similarly, membership of BITC, and other charitable/business organisations should be considered as this brings considerable opportunity to showcase CCI activity – for example BITC runs programmes called 'Seeing is Believing' where business leaders visit examples of good CCI practice. Such organisations present networking opportunities to raise the profile of a company's CCI with opinion formers from political, charitable and commercial groups.

Celebrities

Celebrity involvement is a tried and trusted way of encouraging media interest in a CCI campaign. Celebrities can either be chosen on the basis that they have a real life connection, or they can be selected simply because they are the media's popular choice at the moment.

Celebrities can be useful for national media launches, as well as regional media events. They can bring an element of glamour to employee events and at visits to locations which involve the people who are being helped by the CCI activity – schools, hostels, etc

As with all celebrities, clear and firm contractual agreements will be needed to confirm what is expected of them and what the charges will be.

Surveys on the cause

Surveys are a tried and trusted way to generate media coverage, and this technique is equally applicable in the area of CCI. Typically surveys could be conducted into public awareness of the issue being supported by the CCI campaign. The survey could be conducted either by your charitable partner, or an acknowledged expert in the field, in order to add credibility to the announcement of results.

As with all PR in this area, it will be important to weave the name and role of your company into the story about the survey results. It is clearly essential to convey the message that your

organisation is supporting this cause and why. For this element of the story to survive the editing process, managers must work closely with their PR advisors to determine a credible rationale for why a journalist should include the company in any report of a survey of this nature.

The charitable partner can also help to steer media interest towards the company in addition to themselves. The company involvement will be more likely to be covered if it is based on an involvement which goes beyond simply providing cash. It is far more newsworthy for the company behind the CCI to have some vested interest in tackling the issue. For example, a company may choose to support the fight against ageism, because it is keen to recruit older staff.

These are just some of the fundamental ways in which a company can develop publicity for its CCI. Typically it is harder to sell a good news story, which is why CCI publicity needs to be creative and eye catching.

More and more companies are applying the same levels of marketing and PR expertise to this area and with caution, there is no reason why your CCI activity should not become a key component of your corporate or brand reputation, as long as sufficient resource – both financial and in terms of quality of thought – is applied from the outset.

Evaluation of PR activity

It is not the role of this briefing to cover in detail the methods of evaluation for PR programmes that are in place to support CCI activity.

There is considerable work being conducted by the PR industry into evaluation methods and PR practitioners, both within companies and in consultancies, can work together with charities to develop an evaluation system that is effective for the individual CCI campaigns involved.

Best practice in the area of evaluating CCI can be sourced from organisations such as BITC or the London Benchmarking Group. Again both organisations can provide significant written material and practical assistance.

Audience research – consumer, employee and opinion former as relevant – is also strongly recommended to track levels of awareness of CCI over time as part of a general view of favourability towards the company.

This evaluation should be critically linked to the objectives set and agreed at the development stage of the CCI activity.

Evaluation seems, from the research for this briefing, to be a very well established part of the CCI landscape. 57 per cent of the companies surveyed complete media evaluation and 43 per cent use research of target audiences to track the impact of their CCI. Although, overall

this is positive, evaluation seems to be an area where one might quite reasonably expect to see figures in the 90s, given the amount of debate and apparent commitment to evaluation one hears in business circles.

Companies can also buy into multi-client, cost effective studies of corporate reputation that run regularly – MORI, Research International and several other leading research firms run such studies at least annually.

It is certainly worth including some sets of questions around the impact of favourable corporate citizenship and purchasing behaviour in any ongoing consumer and opinion former research that is already planned.

There is also existing data which can provide a useful template. For example, research carried out in July 1998 by The Future Foundation of consumer attitudes to corporate citizenship is fascinating and well worth reading. The two key points to note are the link between the consumers' perception of how good a corporate citizen a company was, and how closely that correlated with consumer loyalty and satisfaction.

According to The Future Foundation research, where people rated a company highly as a good corporate citizen, they were more likely to buy its products rather than a competitor's and their reported levels of satisfaction were higher than for products purchased from companies with a lower rating as a good corporate citizen.

This is one of the few pieces of research which I have come across, which begins to measure the causal links between good corporate citizenship and sales and it would be pleasing to see more companies include such questions in their evaluation research.

Whatever evaluation method a company chooses, I believe that evaluation is a responsibility that every manager should try and live up to. Not only is it good business practice, but it helps the good causes to know how to improve and refine their fundraising and campaigning activity.

But perhaps most importantly, the effort to evaluate as thoroughly and professionally as possible, is essential if CCI is to become accepted by the business community, as a core business function that can add real value. Unless CCI practitioners take the evaluation responsibility seriously, they will always be highly exposed and more prone than most to an uncertain future within the corporate entity.

CCI case studies – inspiration from three do right companies

Unilever plc

Diageo plc

McDonald's Restaurants Ltd and the millennium 'our town story'

chapter 7

Chapter 7:
CCI case studies – inspiration from three do right companies

Unilever plc

Unilever's long term commitment to responsible corporate behaviour is fundamental to its operating tradition. The company believes strongly that due to the nature of its products – which are used by millions of consumers many times throughout every day, all over the world – the business must conduct itself in a way that reflects its integral role in everyday life.

Unilever recognises that consumers and employees are also citizens and that they will view the company and its brands using a set of values based on societal structures, traditions and prevailing viewpoints.

This philosophy of the importance to be in tune with the social wavelength in each market, is reflected in the decentralised nature of the business. Local Unilever companies are predominately run by local people, who are part of that society.

To be accepted in a country, it is clearly vital for Unilever to be a good corporate citizen. This primarily involves providing consumer benefit and wealth creation through the production of safe and effective products. However, in addition, the company believes strongly in making a contribution to improving the societal structure of each market.

This is centrally guided by the Corporate Relations and External Affairs Committee of Advisory Directors, which produces best practice guidelines and world-wide operation standards for a range of corporate activities, including CCI and issues relating to social responsibility. The Committee is also charged with providing evaluation and continuous improvement processes for CCI. As with its brands and entire corporate philosophy, Unilever's CCI must always be based on a close understanding of the needs of the societies in which it operates and should meet society's evolving expectations of corporate behaviour.

Reflecting its multi-local global position, CCI projects are chosen by Unilever's local businesses, who are in the best position to reflect the expectations and needs of that market. Global themes are suggested by the centre, but there is no directive, other than on standards of integrity.

Unilever describes its CCI activity as 'helping at the edges'. It does not replace national government responsibility, but it does seek to address specific areas of need in each country – naturally

this will vary dramatically, from providing clean drinking water in a developing country, to helping raise standards of education – one of the key themes in the UK, for example.

Unilever takes note of the agendas of national governments when considering what to support, but is not driven by them. The primary drivers for what issues the CCI activity should address reflects three key factors:

1. The skills (in addition to funding) that the business is able to offer to society – eg intellectual expertise and managerial experience

2. Themes relevant to the individual brand positionings

3. Shared areas, where the interests of Unilever are also the interests of society.

Three examples of where Unilever's interests and those of society have been addressed by CCI, are in water management, sustainable fishing and education.

Water is crucial to the way many Unilever products are made and consumed, and it is clearly a very important resource that is under threat across the world. Unilever is developing a set of guidelines with Forum for the Future, which will help operating companies choose local CCI schemes which focus on sustainable water management. In this way Unilever is working within society to help tackle this issue together with all stakeholders.

Similarly, Unilever formed the Marine Stewardship Council with the World Wildlife Fund for Nature as a group dedicated to promoting sustainable fishing methods. Like the water management theme, Unilever has a significant business interest in ensuring there are sufficient and sustainable stocks of fish left in the world, in order to continue using its production facilities for fish products. Similarly, society needs to ensure there is adequate fish available to eat as it provides a nutritious diet for millions around the world, in addition to contributing towards local economic activity.

Unilever's CCI in education is another example of a common area of interest between the company and society – for Unilever, high educational standards help to provide a well educated workforce, and a more stable economy and socio-political environment in which to make long term business decisions. For society and the citizens within it, better education brings enhanced opportunities and an edge in a competitive global economy.

For Unilever, CCI should aim to be seen as the company's contribution towards solving a shared issue – reflecting the corporate philosophy of being part of society, not apart from it. Unilever is clearly one of the leading proponents of inside out company thinking, which puts society and its citizen consumers at the heart of the business.

Other examples of Unilever company CCI initiatives around the world include Vandenburgh Foods' Nutrition Education Project in Natal, South Africa, which teaches school children the basic requirements of a healthy diet and which encourages the plantation of highly productive, small vegetable patches using recycled household waste as compost. In addition, the company provides funding, logistical and managerial support, plus educational materials.

A project in India supported by Hindustan Lever to help improve milk yields for cattle farmers, is another project which attempts to reverse poor quality and erratic milk production. Unilever supports an integrated programme designed to help farmers improve the efficiency of their operations through better animal husbandry, diversification, infrastructure improvement, training and education.

In the UK, Unilever is helping schools to achieve Investors in People status. The company is providing employee involvement with schools plus other more general assistance, to help schools apply for and pass the standard. The company also helps to make IIP more affordable for schools, through the provision of sponsorship funding, and practical assistance from local companies.

Implementation is delivered in partnerships between Training and Enterprise Councils (which are based all over the UK) and local Unilever operating companies such as Birds Eye Wall's, Colmans of Norwich, Elida Faberge, Lever Brothers and Van den Bergh Foods. This initiative is part of a larger commitment to education in the UK, which has four key themes of:

- Business awareness and enterprise
- Science and technology
- School management and leadership (where the Investors In People scheme fits)
- Business – Education Partnership.

In Turkey, Unilever's surface cleaning brand, Cif, supported a campaign to clean up significant national buildings and public spaces in 23 cities across Turkey. A specially branded steam train would arrive in each city to mark the beginning of each phase of the campaign. Local monuments, central parks, and main streets were selected in conjunction with local municipalities and council bodies for cleaning. Cif provided the funding required to restore these high profile community landmarks. The campaign, which ran over two years, clearly linked to the core brand values and helped to build integration of the business into everyday life within local communities.

Unilever produces a range of excellent written publications on its CCI activities around the world, which show how CCI has been used as a core business tool to deliver competitive commercial edge through the support of real social issues, that touch the company's employees and consumers on an everyday basis.

Diageo plc

Diageo is a global owner of famous brands including Burger King, Guinness, Green Giant, Smirnoff, and J&B whisky. The company focuses on alcoholic drinks and food products in the main.

As well as a leader in global brand development, Diageo is also acknowledged as one of the most sophisticated and committed supporters of Corporate Community Investment and Corporate Social Responsibility.

Diageo sees CCI as a core part of corporate citizenship – an area it takes seriously, with a full time Director of Corporate Citizenship. Diageo commits 1 per cent of its annual worldwide trading profits to support local community activity. CCI activity is developed to be an expression of one of Daigeo's core values, which is 'freedom to succeed'.

The company has formed the Diageo Foundation to be a vehicle that supports charitable organisations which support the 'freedom to succeed' theme. The Foundation concentrates on the following areas:

- Our people – matching employee fundraising efforts and payroll giving up to a maximum of £1,500 and £1,200 per employee per year respectively.

- Water of life – an international humanitarian and environmental initiative supporting water related projects.

- Skills for life – designed to help people of all ages and cultures develop skills to improve their quality of life

- Local citizens – focusing on regeneration of communities around Diageo business locations with the aim of tackling issues such as homelessness and unemployment. The company also looks to support local culture and community based arts in communities local to the business's operations.

The Foundation considers appeals from charitable organisations and lists its preferences as follows:

- Excluded and disadvantaged people who, with support, can help themselves to transform their own lives

- Partnerships with community groups rather than individuals

- Locations where the company operates

- Where the Foundation's involvement can make a difference

- Kick start funding to get Diageo employees and business units involved.

All funding has a three year time limit applied. Local operating companies are encouraged to get involved in Foundation supported initiatives and to actively promote their involvement through publicity opportunities. Evaluation is rigorous in identifying effectiveness and benefits delivered to both the community and to Diageo. Interestingly Diageo stresses the importance of its CCI being measured by what is achieved rather than what is given – impact rather than output.

The Diageo Foundation overlays and supports the operating companies, who can choose to support Foundation led programmes or develop their own initiatives.

The company has a pragmatic approach to how its operating companies get involved. The Foundation and the central CCI team are there to help and encourage, but country markets are free to develop their own initiatives. The important thing is that each market does something and that it is then implemented to a high standard. Diageo is less concerned about imposing centralised themes and strictures and more concerned about enabling its businesses to be good corporate citizens in a way that is relevant to their market and societies.

Global differences present a challenge and the central CCI team spend a considerable amount of effort in encouraging countries where CCI is less established, to get involved in a way that is suitable for the business and for that market's needs.

Diageo is keen to let local businesses take the recognition and credit for their CCI activity, and does not overtly brand CCI initiatives in local markets with the Diageo brand – preferring to let the consumer facing brand take the credit. Central assistance is more in the background, providing ideas and advice on good procedures and effective campaign management.

For Diageo, CCI is part of the bigger desire to be a good corporate citizen. The company wants to be seen as a force for good that takes its responsibilities seriously. This building of a reputation for being responsible is especially useful for Diageo, given that it is a major producer of alcoholic drinks, which can attract controversy. A positive corporate reputation provides a far more substantive platform from which to debate such issues and is likely to help the company trade these products in a sustainable way.

For Diageo, CCI is part of earning its licence to operate. The company uses CCI at a corporate level to support its goals, but also to assist its operating businesses and brands. Diageo's local businesses in turn use CCI to address local social issues and to boost individual brand values – helping to build consumer loyalty, satisfaction and added sales in many cases.

McDonald's Restaurants Ltd and the millennium 'our town story'

McDonald's commitment to support the businesses in which it operates is a central principle, which dates back to the start of the company. Founder Ray Kroc believed strongly that the business should put something back into the community from which it derives its customers, employees and suppliers. McDonald's has, ever since, sought to carry out CCI activity which reflects its role as a local restaurant – even if it is part of a global brand – making the restaurant part of the community, with the staff playing a key role in getting involved in community based CCI.

The guiding principles for the company in the UK are to:

- Become synonymous with helping young people in need

- Contribute one per cent of pre tax profits to the community

- Support initiatives that support grass roots activity

- Provide premises, products and people to support the community and charitable fundraising

- Encourage employee volunteering, using company time and facilities where possible

- Assist charities with McDonald's' training skills

- Be active members of business organisations responsible for encouraging corporate social responsibly

- Encourage community involvement through senior leadership and integration of community involvement in management development

- Regularly monitor and review CCI activity

- Tell stakeholders about the company's CCI initiatives.

In the UK, McDonald's social responsibility programme is focused on the following core areas:

- children and child welfare

- the family

- education

- health

- the environment

- youth related social issues.

The company has a very active programme of CCI that is delivered all around the UK, with strong and professional guidance and assistance from the centre. CCI is truly integrated into

the culture of the company, with all members of staff becoming involved and seeing CCI as a key part of their personal career development.

The CCI programmes range from very high profile big events such as Mc Happy Day and the Big Smile Appeal, which are locally based fundraising activities, through to a whole range of support given to local community projects from youth football sponsorship to supporting youth development and environmental improvement programmes with the Groundwork Trust.

The principal vehicle for fundraising in the UK is Ronald McDonald Children's Charities Limited, which is an independent charity funded by the company to contribute funds – both corporate donations and fund raised monies – to charities which benefit children. Probably the most well known example of the type of support provided are the Ronald McDonald Houses, which provide accommodation for families with children suffering from serious and long term illness.

McDonald's provides an excellent range of literature giving full details on its CCI policies, philosophy and activities. However, the company's latest CCI scheme is not currently in the published literature. This is McDonald's' support of the New Millennium Experience's Our Town Story programme.

This is the company's major support project for the Millennium. The 'our town story' programme involves every Local Education Authority. Each LEA is tasked with nominating a combined grouping of two or three schools from within their area. The schools will work with the New Millennium Experience and McDonald's throughout 1999, to create a stage play that tells the story of their local town and which talks about what the future might be like for that community.

The performance will then be given by the schoolchildren at the Millennium Dome in Greenwich throughout 2000. The performances will also be given in the local community where the schools are based.

The programme is related to the national curriculum and supports areas such as history. McDonald's' involvement in this initiative will include grass roots support such as employees helping with rehearsals, providing restaurants for meetings and funding coaches to take children to the Dome to carry out their performances. The company is also funding the project co-ordination carried out by the Local Education Authorities – vital given the limited resources to take on extra work within the typical LEA.

McDonald's will treat this as one of its major community projects for the next two years and is hoping that Our Town Story will enable the local restaurants to make an even bigger contribution towards local community activities for the Millennium and beyond.

Appendix

Bibliography

Appendix

Bibliography

1. Cannibals with forks: John Elkington

2. BP in the UK Community: produced by BP

3. Sustainability Advisory Services: produced by KPMG

4. Partnerships with Business: produced by The Department for International Development of Her Majesty's UK Government

5. Insight into cause marketing, by Yasmeen Khan, reproduced in Marketing Week, 26 February 1998

6. Time for business to take an ethical stand: PR Week, 11 December 1998

7. Does corporate social responsibility matter to the City: produced by MORI, December 1998

8. Examples of excellence in Corporate Community Investment: Business in the Community

9. CWS Community Dividend application form and leaflet: produced by The Co-op

10. Forum Briefing: Produced by The Prince of Wales Business Leaders Forum – Autumn 1998 issue

11. Corporate Citizenship – business and community: seven case studies, produced by High Life magazine, Autumn 1998

12. Cause Related Marketing – The Charities Perspective: produced by Countrywide Porter Novelli, January 1999

13. VanCity's Social Report 1997: Produced by VanCity

14. Connecting with the Community: video produced by Grand Metropolitan, 1997

15. Corporate Citizenship Review: South African Breweries Limited, 31 March, 1998

16. The Business Case for Giving: MORI, 3 December 1998

17. Charity to run first privatised school: Article in The Times, January 1999

18. Three things matter in business: reputation, reputation and reputation: Article in The Observer, 22 November 1998

19. The Partnership report: The Co-operative Bank, March 1998

20. So what are we doing about it?: Railtrack corporate responsibility review 1997/98

21. Community Review: produced by United Utilities

22. Corporate Citizenship: produced by The Future Foundation and The Consumers' Association, July 1998

23. Cause to talk: produced by Countrywide Porter Novelli

24. Social accountability: produced by BVQI

25. Business in the community – a Financial Times Guide, 3 December 1998

26. Playing our part in the community: a review of Camelot's charitable support across the UK, produced by Camelot plc

27. Brushing up our communities (August 1998); Helping children reach for the sky (July 1996); Ronald McDonald Children's Charities newsletter (June 1998); Every picture tells a story (June 1998): all produced by McDonald's Restaurants Limited

28. Diageo Foundation; produced by Diageo plc

29. Unilever magazine (numbers 103 and 110); A sense of community (February 1997); Unilever Magazine (South Africa, December 1998); Unilever Foundation for Education & Development – meeting the needs of South Africa's people; Securing the future of the seafood industry (15 September 1998); Sustainability: Unilever's approach (March 1997); Unilever support for education in the UK(September 1997); Raising standards through Investors in People in schools – evaluation summary (Autumn 1998): All produced by Unilever plc

30. Business as partners in development: produced by The Prince of Wales Business Leaders Forum in collaboration with The World Bank and The United Nations Development Programme

31. MORI's annual Corporate Social Responsibility Study, 1998